Student's Guide to Finding a Superior Job

March, 1995

To Daniel,
Here's wishing you the outstanding job you deserve!
Ariane

Student's Guide to Finding a Superior Job

Second Edition

William A. Cohen

Amsterdam • Johannesburg • London
San Diego • Sydney • Toronto

Pfeiffer & Company
8517 Production Avenue
San Diego, CA 92121-2280 USA

Library of Congress Cataloging in Publication Data

Cohen, William A.
The student's guide to finding a superior job.

1. Job hunting. 2. College graduates - Employment
3. Students - Employment. 1. Title
HF5382.7.C64 1987 650. 1'4 87-4487

ISBN 0-89384-200-1

Text set in 12.5-point Bodoni Antiqua Light

Printed in the United States of America.
1 2 3 4 5 6 7 8 9 10

Dedication

To my students, past, present, and future,
who have demonstrated time and time again
their abilities to obtain superior jobs
and perform them well.

Contents

Introduction

Your techniques made my short-lived experiences as valuable to a company as an MBA.

Some years ago I wrote a book, *The Executive's Guide to Finding a Superior Job*, based in part on my experiences as an executive recruiter. This book proved to be a bestseller and a phenomenal success in helping managers, executives, and other professionals to obtain jobs. The letters I received led me to consider how university students could apply the same techniques. I began to tailor my job-finding techniques for students and to teach these techniques in my marketing classes in a special lecture called "Self-Marketing."

Once again, the results achieved with these techniques proved truly phenomenal. One student's comment typifies others: "As an undergraduate, just beginning to enter the job market, your techniques made my short-lived experiences as valuable to a company as an MBA ."

One student, a foreign national, succeeded in getting a job as a management consultant with an American firm, even though his degree was from a so-called second-tiered school. His starting salary was one of the highest ever achieved by a graduate from the school in question.

Another student, with a year or two of experience, translated her degree into a starting position as director of advertising with a well-known clothing manufacturer. Another high point was reached when a former student called to say that, using her MBA as an entree, she had received a starting salary of $55,000. Certainly this had to rank among the top one percent of starting salaries in America.

As my business students became more successful using the techniques I taught, students from other academic backgrounds began to call and I was asked to speak before several groups about finding jobs. Would the same techniques work for, say, English, anthropology, or art majors? The answer is a definite yes. The techniques are not peculiar to business or to marketing. They work regardless of discipline and regardless of academic background.

Why Old-fashioned Job-Finding Techniques Won't Work

There was a time when the techniques used by ninety-nine percent of graduating students really worked. The students who used them found reasonably good jobs. This was, however, a period when college graduates were in great demand, regardless of background and specialty. In truth, almost anyone could find a good job, and almost everyone who used the old techniques was successful.

The techniques I'm speaking of include the traditional services provided by schools, such as inviting recruiters from large companies to come to the campus to interview students. Can you get a job this way today? The answer is yes, with two caveats:

- Not every student is hired as a result of this interviewing process. You must be one of the lucky few.
- The job that you get using these methods is one of the usual entry-level jobs companies offer to recent graduates. It is a superior job relative only to other entry-level jobs.

For example, if your definition of a superior job involves high compensation, you should know that most companies do not anticipate paying $55,000 for a newly minted master's degree.

There are other reasons why the old techniques are no longer sufficient for obtaining really good jobs. In marketing terms, perhaps the biggest reason is that these techniques fail to employ what we call the marketing concept.

The marketing concept does not focus on what you want to sell, but on the customer's requirements–the customer in this case is your potential employer.

According to the marketing concept, a student who works up a resume based on experiences relating to a particular subject, has it printed, and mails it to potential employers is 100 percent wrong. The employer is very interested in the student's other experiences. Locked into what the student thinks are his best features, the employer inevitably offers an average entry-level job, or no job at all.

Another reason old-fashioned techniques no longer work is that they don't address the segmentation of the market. In the old days, to put job finding in marketing terms again, one did "mass marketing," which means that the one doing the marketing attempted to sell to everyone. Today, marketers are much more sophisticated. Rather than trying to be everything to everybody, they attempt to segment the market based on certain common characteristics of that segment. By concentrating on satisfying the needs of the segment they target, they are much more likely to be successful.

Using the old job-finding methods rather than market segmentation can result in competition among friends from your own school, academic major, or university and students from universities all over your geographic area, and possibly from all over the country. You, your classmates, and thousands of others, are actually competing for a very small number of positions. The results obtained from positioning yourself correctly within a certain market segment of potential employers will amaze you.

Finally, the old-fashioned job techniques won't work in today's world because they do not allow you to concentrate your superior and unique qualifications against your competition in order to win a superior job.

How This Book Will Help You Find a Superior Job

Before reading this book, scan it to see how the book will help you to find a superior job. Here are the specific ways in which the book does this:

- You learn four actions to take as a student that have nothing to do with grade point average or studying, but that double your worth to a potential employer.
- You discover ten ways to develop a detailed and superior resume and make it work for you by not sending it to anyone.
- You learn how to locate superior jobs by job title, position in the company, industry, geographical location, and company size. You also learn to identify your future boss, by name, even before you seek an interview.
- You are taught the most effective promotional techniques you can use to bypass personnel and human resource people and to force your future boss to hire you directly.
- You are given two keys that enable you to control the interview and that make you the outstanding candidate for any position.

- Finally, you learn how to obtain, negotiate, and decide among several simultaneous superior job opportunities.

After reading this book you can expect to:

- Obtain more quality interviews than you ever thought possible. As one of my students, Michael Ginsberg, said, "The response from the thirty-nine letters I sent to top executives of computer sales companies was so tremendous that I could not keep up with the demand. The firms were inviting me back for further interviews."
- Be sought after and wanted, sometimes desperately, by several potential employers.
- Have several excellent job opportunities to select from at the same time.
- Achieve a superior job.

1 ONE

Actions to Take Before Looking for a Job

Grades count for a very small part of your ability to find a superior job. Many other things that you do as a student will help far more.

There are a number of actions you can take while still a student that will help you find a superior job. Most students think good grades are the only key. However, the fact of the matter is that grades count for a very small part of your ability. Many other things that you do as a student will help far more.

Some of these actions are automatic, and you will do them anyway. You need only realize that you are doing them and how they will assist in the job search. Other actions that take very little effort can have an amazingly large impact on your ability to succeed with the job-finding campaign. And, finally, a few actions will require a lot of effort, but their results will be well worth it, putting you years ahead of your classmates when it comes to your paycheck and job satisfaction. Let's look at each of these actions.

Selection of Courses

Which courses you take can play a very important part in your job search. Of course, if you are already on your last quarter or semester, you may have very little choice in this respect. But, if you do have a choice, certain courses will be more beneficial than others, depending on the components of your superior job or in the general business field that interests you. Obviously, if you are an English major who has thought about journalism as a career, a course in journalism would clearly be of benefit. In the same vein, at some point while working toward your degree in history, you may decide that marketing is of interest. Don't be afraid of taking a course in marketing.

But you should know right from the start that it's important to get contacts in your area of interest.

Taking additional business courses outside your primary specialty may provide help in clinching the deal for your superior job and will expose you to contacts in your field of business that you can use later in your job search. I will be talking more later about these contacts and how you can find and develop a mutually beneficial relationship with them. But you should know right from the start that it's important to get contacts in your area of interest. Even as a freshman or sophomore, as you develop certain interests and consider certain types of careers, you should take courses in those areas so that you will meet the contacts that are likely to be useful.

Extracurricular Activities

Extracurricular activities are also important. Much more so than you may have thought. These activities include participation in hobby groups, student government and councils, working on faculty committees as a student, tutoring other students, and joining clubs, associations, sororities or fraternities.

Again, I want to stress that contacts are important, and you will meet many business contacts while engaging in extracurricular activities who will be important to your job-finding campaign on graduation. However, extracurricular activities have an even more important benefit. Participation in them will allow you to undertake projects and to accomplish tasks that will be of great interest to prospective employers.

While engaging in extracurricular activities, you will meet many business contacts who will be important to your job-finding campaign.

All positions of leadership and responsibility, such as president, vice president, or secretary of associations, clubs, sororities, fraternities, and so forth, demonstrate your ability to lead. Temporary leadership positions, including chairperson of a committee for ticket sales, are equally beneficial. Look at some of the actual student letters reprinted in Chapter Five and you will see many examples of students who have accomplished specific, perhaps one-time projects while participating in extracurricular activities that directly support their goals to become salespeople, accountants, office managers, and virtually every superior job in the business and not-for-profit world.

So participate in extracurricular activities. Participate as leader in as many as you can handle. And don't forget to note what you did and what the results of your efforts were. Some of these achievements can be reclaimed later when you prepare a detailed resume–the resume that you will not send to anyone–that you'll use to get incredibly good interviews. Better yet, record your activities as they happen, along with your accomplishments, and quantify everything as discussed in the chapters on developing your resume and sales letter.

Finally, extracurricular activities provide yet another benefit that will help you find and obtain a truly superior job, right out of school. Participating in a variety of these activities is a demonstration of a well-rounded individual. At the same time, participating in a variety of activities will help overcome negative images a prospective employer may have if your grades are somewhat poor.

In fact, it is a good answer to the question as to why you don't have higher grades. Indicate that you participated in many different activities you felt would be of benefit to your education. Then you can proceed to talk about your extracurricular activities and why they would help you perform well in the superior job for which you are a candidate. This approach will immediately turn the negative image into a positive.

Internships, Part-time and Summer Jobs

Even if you do not receive payment for working while attending school, there are a variety of other benefits. These are the same benefits that are available from extracurricular activities–and for many of the same reasons. As with extracurricular activities, part-time jobs, summer jobs, and internships provide an opportunity to show what you can do in the real world while undertaking your academic work.

They provide the opportunity to do tasks that are accomplishments. Did you make an extraordinary number of sales as a part-time shoe salesperson? This achievement can be very important if you want a superior job as a salesperson. Did you assist in a hospital or in some social welfare program? For different types of jobs this experience can be equally important. All of the things that you do as a student–part-time, full-time, or in an internship–are valid accomplishments.

Many employers will be interested in hearing about these accomplishments because they relate directly to your ability to accomplish similar work. These statements of results will assist a prospective employer in deciding that you are an outstanding candidate for a superior job.

Part-time jobs, summer jobs, and internships provide an opportunity for you to show what you can do in the real world.

You may wonder about internships that pay little or nothing. Is it really worth it? Most definitely yes, if the work is in the area of your job interest. When we get to the advertising phase of your job-finding campaign, you will very clearly see that it is not a matter of payment, but rather what you have actually accomplished. Therefore, internships in your area of interest can be of tremendous value whether or not you are paid in dollars and cents.

Again, as with courses and extracurricular activities, all types of part-time, full-time, summer jobs, and internships are a source of contacts for you. These contacts may be very useful later on. Employers are sometimes so impressed with the work students do in part-time jobs and internships that they hire them after graduation. Also, your employer may know of other superior jobs that you may be interested in while a student. Finally, assuming that you do a good job, these employers are outstanding job references, above and beyond friends, relatives, and professors, since the recommendations of past employers are usually given more weight than those of people who would be expected to give you a good recommendation.

Guest Speaker Contacts

Guest speakers who come to your school to speak before large groups or before a single class can be very important contacts for you, and you should never let the opportunity go by to:

- Favorably impress the speaker, whenever possible.
- Obtain the speaker's name, address, telephone number, and company name.

- Jot down important facts about the speaker and what he or she said, as well as questions you may have asked about the speaker's presentation.

Of course, after the presentation is over, you should always take the time to meet the speaker personally, shake hands, and further discuss the subject of the speech. If you have a particular interest in working in the speaker's area of expertise, be sure to make it known.

Never be afraid to ask the speaker questions, even pointed questions about the type of job that interests you, the industry, the work, or what the prospects are for working in the industry after your graduation. Always be pleasant and tactful. Remember that you want to be on good terms with the speaker and make a favorable impression.

Speaker contacts can be very useful just before graduation. This is when you will begin to gather more detailed and pertinent information about the industry and, more specifically, the type of job you are seeking. Occasionally, speakers who remember you because of your questions, or because you went out of your way to make a favorable impression, may be able to assist you directly in finding a superior job.

Sometimes speakers may take a particular interest and help a student obtain a part-time summer job or internship in the company where the speaker works. This contact is of immeasurable and invaluable assistance prior to graduation, and in getting a superior job after graduation.

Your Studies As a Source of Contacts

Every class assignment is another opportunity for contacts who can help you find a superior job. For example, doing a report in a particular industry gives you the opportunity to talk directly to top managers in that industry. This would be very difficult once you graduate and are no longer a student. But many managers, even senior company officers, are willing to talk with you as a student and to help you get information useful to your studies.

All you do is telephone the company that interests you and ask the receptionist for the name of the manager. The receptionist will then connect you with the manager's secretary. Tell the secretary that you are a student and that you would like to interview the manager for a report you are doing. When you talk to the executive, be courteous and pleasant and clearly explain what you want and why. Ask if you can have an appointment for a fifteen-minute interview. Once this has been scheduled, prepare for the interview by reading everything you can about the industry. It is important that the executive's time is not wasted with questions that could have been answered by a visit to any library.

This preparation also demonstrates that you have invested time and effort before the interview and, of course, allows you to make a favorable impression on the executive. When you go for the appointment, make certain that you are on time and dressed appropriately. Many so-called short, fifteen-minute interviews have turned into interviews of an hour or longer, and a few even result in superior job offers upon graduation.

But again, what you are trying to do here is establish friendships and contacts in a certain area of interest. These interviews will help you decide if a company, industry, or type of work is really what you want. Sometimes through an interview you will meet other company managers who will be good targets for your sales letter campaign later.

The information you obtain about the industry, as well as the contacts and information sources you cultivate, enables you to create a high profile with different companies, an invaluable asset even as a student. You are missing valuable opportunities if you have not been taking advantage of your classroom assignments in this way.

How the Small Business Institute Can Help

The Small Business Institute (SBI) is a small business consulting program run by students who are supervised by professors. It is sponsored by the Small Business Administration of the United States federal government. It usually operates out of the School of Business at most major universities. Small businesses need consulting services as much as large ones, but frequently cannot afford the large consulting fees.

The Small Business Administration has the task of helping small businesses. One way it does this is with a program in which a university uses students as consultants. They are supervised by their professors. The students consult with the small business client on real business problems: marketing, finance, accounting, management, and so forth.

Involvement in this program could be of tremendous value when you are seeking a superior job. Sometimes the owner of a client company wants to hire a recent graduate. Because the firm is small, the job might be for a top manager of the company, a director, a manager, or a vice president. Such a high-ranking job is possible because many small firms cannot afford to hire a high-priced, experienced executive. If you have experience in the functional area of the small business, this type of job offer can be a tremendous opportunity even if the compensation isn't great. After all, an initial job as a top manager, even for a small company, is nothing to sneeze at.

But working as a consultant in the Small Business Institute program has other major job-finding advantages. Perhaps the best of these is that you are actually acting as a business consultant, solving real business problems, an opportunity few students have prior to graduation. Consultants–and those that do consulting–have a mystique that is held in high respect by many managers in industry. Your accomplishments as a consultant and the positive results of your recommendations to the small business client can have a very significant impact on convincing prospective employers of your worth when you are seeking your superior job.

Another advantage of working with the SBI program is that universities usually give academic credit for your consulting efforts. If you are interested in this program, I would recommend that you contact the School of Business at your university or college and ask about the SBI program and its requirements. Even if you are required to take one or two additional courses first, or to have upper-division standing, the program is well worth it. The experience, contacts, and the consulting background that such an effort provides will help you find a superior job.

How Professors Can Help

In addition to providing academic instruction, professors can offer other assistance in your job search. They are a good source of contacts if you are interested in certain types of work, industries, or companies, and they will often be happy to introduce you to people if you approach them courteously and ask for their help. But in addition, professors may also be able to help by giving you their paid or nonpaid research assistant assignments. These can be of great value when listing your accomplishments.

However, it's important not to take just any research assignment for a professor, or to take a job with *any* professor as a research assistant. Rather, try to get a job in an area that interests you and can support your case for a superior job later.

Contact professors in the areas of your academic studies with whom you have developed a rapport. However, do not be afraid to approach professors with whom you have not studied but who work in your area of interest. You do not need to limit yourself to your discipline of study. For example, although you may be a liberal arts student, nothing prevents you from approaching a professor in some other school, such as engineering or business.

Professors are a good source of contacts if you are interested in certain types of work, industries, or companies.

The key to success is how you approach the professor. Of course, if you know a professor, you can ask him or her to introduce you to another that you do not know. In any case, always be polite, courteous, make an appointment ahead of time, and understand that the professor is doing you a favor when he or she assists you. Of course, some professors will help more than others, and some professors will not help at all. You should recognize this fact ahead of time and not let it bother you as you seek help. Fortunately, there are enough helpful professors around, so you should have little trouble finding plenty who are willing to help. Some may even give you work.

If all else fails, become a nonpaid research assistant. The title is the same, and it is the long-term benefits that you are primarily after. Some professors will give you academic credit for your work in lieu of pay. Never be afraid to ask, the worse that can happen is that you'll get a no.

How to Develop Contacts in Any Company

Being a student puts you in a unique position that you will not enjoy again at any other time in your working career. It allows you to make a "cold" contact in any company or in any industry–not to ask them directly about a job, but to ask them about the industry or the potential for a job in that industry or company.

For example, let's say that you are interested in getting a job as a graphic artist in the advertising industry. While still a student, nothing prevents you from phoning an advertising agency and finding out from the receptionist who is the president of the firm. You can then ask for the president by name and indicate that you are a student with a strong interest in advertising and graphic arts and ask for advice on how to train yourself for a job in that industry. It's important that you make it clear that you are not presently looking for a job. Do this early enough in your career as a student, that is, before you are a senior, so it is clear and self-evident. Using this and similar techniques, you can approach almost anyone you want. Many people, even celebrities, will be ready to talk with you. Perhaps not everyone, but certainly many more than you would imagine.

A variation of this technique is to write to authors of books in the area of your business interest. If you are truly interested in the subject, many authors will help because you share a common interest. One of my former students, while still early in his college career, became the confidant–as well as the assistant–of a very successful science fiction literary agent. At the same time he was able to meet and personally know virtually every major author who had written science fiction. All of this was because of his own great interest in the subject and his willingness to write to those individuals whom he knew only from articles in science fiction magazines and books.

And I have to tell you, I've used the technique myself. While barely out of school, I became a personal friend of a famous inventor of air navigational devices and techniques. I wrote a short letter to him after reading an article he had written about navigation.

Never be afraid to make contact either by telephone or mail when you are seeking information or help from individuals. The results will surprise you and will greatly assist in obtaining a superior job. The beauty of most of the recommendations I have made in this chapter is that they may require very little special effort on your part and cost you nothing but a little time. You have seen that you are automatically given opportunities as a student that can be of importance to you as you begin your campaign for a superior job.

2 TWO

Developing a Powerful Resume

*If you send a resume,
as advised by so many well-meaning
individuals in career development,
it will only hurt your chances
of getting a superior job.*

In this chapter you'll learn how to develop an extremely powerful resume documenting your accomplishments in every aspect of your life and work in school. Yet, you won't send this resume to anyone– certainly not the employment department–not even the executive who has the authority to hire you. I am fully aware that this probably goes against every other bit of information you have ever heard about job finding.

Knock-out Factors and How They Can Prevent You From Being Hired

Many people don't realize it, but any job you seek will contain knock-out factors that prevent you from getting the job and from getting the interview. I first learned about knock-out factors when I was a headhunter. One day I received a call from a client who was seeking a petroleum manager. I immediately got out my pencil and paper in order to write down his exact specifications for the job–technically called a "job order."

The problem with a resume is that any resume contains knock-out factors and you, unfortunately, don't know what they are.

These requirements detailed the exact qualities wanted, and the qualities not wanted. the latter are called knock-out factors because they automatically eliminate anyone who has them. One factor that my client was most emphatic about was that no one with industry experience outside of Texas was eligible. He said, "We are located in the Permian Basin. The petroleum manager we hire must have had recent experience down here. Do not send us a candidate who has not had recent experience in the Permian Basin. We don't want him to have experience in California, the Rocky Mountain area, back East, or anywhere else."

I took down the entire list of requirements as well as the list of knock-out factors. Then I began to look for candidates for my prospective client. Two weeks later, after considerable recruiting, I had located three outstanding candidates. All three fit the requirements of the job order by having the required specifications and none of the knock-out factors. I called my client to arrange interviews for the candidates only to learn that someone had already been hired.

"I'm sorry," the client said, "just this morning we hired an outstanding individual and filled the position." Having spent a considerable amount of time locating the three candidates and motivating them for this particular job, I confess I was not overly delighted, particularly since I received payment only if one of my candidates was hired.

Still, it was important to learn what type of manager my client had hired, so I would have a better idea of his real needs in the future. I asked if he would spend a few minutes telling me about the manager he just hired. "Sure," he said, and he began to tell me about the candidate. When we got to experience, it turned out that the new manager had worked mostly in California and had no experience at all in Texas. "But I thought you said that the candidate must have recent experience in the Permian Basin?" I asked. "Oh yes," he said, "that was a requirement. But, you know, this individual happened to wander by and we interviewed him anyway, and he was such an outstanding individual that we just had to make him an offer."

This story can be repeated over and over again by any headhunter. Knock-out factors really will prevent you from getting an interview, but once you meet face-to-face all bets are off. An individual will often get an offer even though he or she had several knock-out factors that would have prevented an interview if the factors had been known beforehand.

The problem with a resume is that any resume contains knock-out factors and you, unfortunately, don't know what they are. Since every job situation is different, certain factors in your background can eliminate you from an interview. However, the same factors may be ignored after a face-to-face meeting.

Why will a prospective employer ignore knock-out factors once he or she has met with you? Stated quite simply, the employer may like you despite the knock-out factors. Or, the employer may perceive some positive factor to be of overriding importance. Headhunters, in explaining this phenomenon of interviewing, say simply, "The chemistry was right."

You Really Don't Know What's Important in Any Particular Job Situation

Until you have interviewed, you really don't know what's important for a particular job situation. Work you may have done for only a couple of hours may be more important than work you have done for a couple of years. Your perception of a title, even one that you have thoroughly researched, may be faulty because each company is different and uses different titles to mean different things.

Several years ago a friend of mine saw an advertisement in a large metropolitan newspaper for a job that seemed to have been made for him. Every requirement fit him perfectly. He prepared a brilliant resume that fulfilled every single requirement of the ad. He mailed it, fully expecting that he would immediately be invited for an interview.

Several weeks passed and nothing happened. So then my friend decided to call the employment department of this large company to find out about the job. Fortunately, he called when the personnel manager was out and only the secretary was available. She had nothing to do and was willing to talk to him. "Whatever happened about the job?" he asked. "You know," she answered, "We received over 300 resumes and not a single one was what the vice president really wanted." He said he thought everything was in the ad. "Well, we couldn't put everything in, and one of the things left out was that our vice president wanted someone who had some experience developing medical products, even though our company isn't normally in that business. We just received instructions to throw all the resumes out, advertise, and start looking all over again."

My friend actually had some limited experience dealing with medical products. Once, when he had been out of work he had consulted with such a firm and assisted in the development of a medical product that turned out to be quite successful. Because this work occupied only a few days of his employment history, he had omitted it from his resume.

My friend wrote a long letter that answered all the job requirements but that also described in some detail his experience and accomplishments in developing medical products. I will show you later in this chapter how he developed this *letter resume*. Within a week he received a call, not from the employment manager but from his prospective boss. "You know," the vice president said, "We looked through over 300 resumes when we advertised, and not a single one matched what we were looking for, and we were just about to advertise again when your resume came in. We would really like to meet you." And so my friend got the interview and, eventually, the job.

This story emphasizes that a few days or even a few hours of work can be of tremendous importance. Yet you can't get everything you've ever done on a resume. You would have to write a book to include all the part-time jobs, extracurricular activities, and other things you did before entering college. And while at college, think of all the additional things you have done in and out of the classroom! But even if you could send a book of your accomplishments, it wouldn't help–think of all the knock-out factors you would unknowingly include!

A Powerful Technique Gets a Better Job

In this chapter, I'll show how to use the resume to create an extremely powerful job-finding technique. A technique that will get you a superior job faster, easier, and more effectively than a resume sent to the employment or human resources department of a company. Once you try this method, I promise that you will never want to go back to sending resumes again–it's just too ineffective and inefficient.

Developing the Detailed Resume You Will Not Send

Even though you don't have your resume professionally typed or printed, and even though it will not be sent to anyone, it is important that you do not rush the job. You need to spend time thinking about everything you have ever done, and noting accomplishments that may interest a prospective employer. Note that I said accomplishments and not experience, there is a difference.

Once you try this method, I promise that you will never want to go back to sending resumes again, it's just too ineffective and inefficient.

It's great that you were president of your fraternity or sorority, but what did you do as president? What occurred as a result of your being president of your fraternity or sorority, or officer of any club or association? Did you sell tickets for charity? That's fine. But it's not enough to say that you sold "a lot" of tickets–you need to indicate how many tickets you sold and in what period of time. Focus your accomplishments by quantifying them with numbers, percentages, or dollar figures.

That's what prospective employers are looking for. Go over everything you have ever done and write down your experience and your accomplishments in the job. Quantify every accomplishment.

When I say that you should not omit anything, I mean it. Include classroom work. Have you done marketing or business plans, special analyses, historical investigations, or any other classroom reports or projects that might be of interest to a prospective employer? Write it down.

Include sorority or fraternity work, volunteer work; and yes, even include the sale of club fund-raising activities. Include everything. Write down what you did, what the accomplishment was, and quantify it in some fashion. If you've actually had part-time or full-time work, so much the better; but you don't need to have had any paid work to be an attractive job candidate for a superior job.

Here are some accomplishments that may be of importance to a prospective employer:

If you are looking for a sales job:

Have you been a part-time sales clerk?

What did you do that was outstanding?

Did you sell more than other people?
How much did you sell?
Did you deliver newspapers?
Did you build your route?
How much was the increase?
How many new customers?

If you are looking for a job in journalism:

Did you interview people for a college newspaper?
How many people did you interview?
Did you write articles?
Where were they published?
How many and how long?
Have you been an editor?
How many people did you supervise?
Did you win any awards?
Did readership increase as a result of your work?

Sit down and work out this data. Think about what you did and then make a quantified estimate.

If you made phone calls for a market survey:

How many phone calls did you make?
How many did you make in one hour?
How many in a day?
How many days did you spend on the project?

Multiply the figures to quantify the accomplishment.

Did you increase efficiency but you don't know by how much? Think of what was happening before and after your accomplishment. Let's say you introduced a new technique that reduced the number of members that quit a student organization every year. Before your accomplishment, 15 quit every year;

afterward, only 7 quit. That's a 53 percent improvement, due to your work!

Accomplishments are far more powerful than just experience. Many students holding positions in student organizations or who work in part- or full-time jobs may actually accomplish very little. If you can describe your accomplishments and make them credible by quantifying, you will be far ahead of your competition.

Clearly, such a resume requires more than just a few hours effort. You must bring all your material together into a comprehensive list, so that you can immediately extract information pertinent to a specific job. And you must be thoroughly familiar with your accomplishments, so that you can confidently discuss them when you get to the firing line of the interview.

Do Not Be Afraid to Use the Word *I*

Many of my students have asked, "Should I take the entire credit for something that was done by a group I headed, or was in?" If the accomplishment would not have come about without your participation, then take the credit. A job-finding situation is not the time to modestly say, "We did it together," or "I was one of a team of people that did it." If the accomplishment would not have occurred without you, you have the right to state "I caused ____________." Do not be afraid to do this, to have the courage to use the word *I*. If the accomplishment, or same degree of success, would have occurred without you, then you have no right to take credit for the accomplishment.

Plan on working on your resume at least a few hours every day for a week. And every day, review the material, making additions or doing the necessary research so that you can quantify all of your accomplishments. Make certain that nothing is left out.

Some students ask: "How far back should I go for accomplishments?" Well, if you were a child genius, I suppose you could go all the way back to a single digit age. However, for most of us, it's enough to start about the time you were in high school. Even these early accomplishments can be of tremendous importance to an employer. Again, remember that even a few days or a few hours of work–when combined with your other accomplishments, qualifications, and experience–could be exactly what your prospective employer is looking for.

Therefore, even accomplishments attained in high school could place you far ahead of your contemporaries in obtaining the superior job that you want.

I want to emphasize an important point: Don't have your resume professionally typed or printed. I say this for two reasons: (1) If you do, you will be tempted to use it. Even though all of the things you have done may appear to be positive, the resume will contain some knock-out factors that will eliminate you from consideration. (2) You will have included too much material. Instead of demonstrating that you're the perfect candidate for the job, your accomplishments and experiences will be spread so thin that you will appear to be a jack-of-all-trades and a master of none.

Do You Ever Send a Resume to Anyone?

In many cases you could be hired without ever sending a formal resume to anyone. This has happened to me and several of my students. But there is one kind of resume that I prepare in almost every case. After an interview I write a personal letter to the individual who interviewed me. If I interviewed with several people, I send the letter to the individual who has the authority to hire me. To develop this letter, I go over the notes I made during the interview. Using these notes, I show how well I meet every requirement that my interviewer said was important.

I'll show you how to do this in Chapter Four. While you might call this a resume, it is actually specifically oriented toward the superior job that I have *already* interviewed for. It is therefore more effective than any professionally printed resume that anyone else could possibly submit *before* an interview.

Spend the time required to make your resume credible. Spend the time to quantify your accomplishments. It will be time well invested and tremendously important to you throughout your job campaign. You will receive one other benefit as well. Every one of us is unique and individual. We have all done certain things that are outstanding. Sometimes it is a combination of things that makes us outstanding.

Regardless, it is this uniqueness that makes us eminently suited to one specific kind of superior job. After you have written down your accomplishments, you can see all the things that you have done. This evidence will improve your self-image and your positive mental attitude tremendously. It will help you possess the confidence and poise that prospective employers can sense in both your written communications and face-to-face interviews. Now, it's important not to waste time. Proceed at once in getting your resume together, even as you read the remainder of this book.

Every one of us is unique.
We have done certain things that are outstanding. That is what makes us eminently suited to one specific kind of superior job.

3

THREE

Market Research and Product Differentiation

Market segmentation allows you to be much stronger in the particular market segment where your superior job lies.

Market research, market segmentation, and product differentiation are marketing concepts that can be directly applied to job-finding campaigns. Market research refers to learning everything you can about the prospective job—or market—and defining what a superior job really is to you. It also refers to learning everything you can about salary, various industries, geographical areas, and size of companies that may interest you.

Market segmentation also has to do with defining your target market. To be most effective, you should focus and concentrate your efforts toward a certain segment of the market you feel is important. By concentrating your resources in one segment, you will be much stronger than your competitors because the other students will be shotgunning their resources over the entire job market.

You will even outclass a student who, in some respects, may be a much stronger candidate. The concept of product differentiation underscores the fact that you are different from everyone else in the world. Therefore, there is a certain job for which you are uniquely—and better—qualified than anyone else.

Pick the right market segment through market research and then differentiate your product (you) from your competition by selecting the right accomplishments from your resume. You can then be confident that you will be perceived as the best candidate for the job you want.

You Must Decide What Constitutes a Superior Job

Only you can decide what a superior job is for you, and you must define it in precise terms. That is, you must define your superior job by industry, by geographical location, by functional area, and by the exact position title, as well as by the amount of compensation you expect.

By defining it, you will be much stronger than your competition who lacks this focus. Your competitors may appear to be keeping their options open by developing career objectives such as, "Any job in which we can make a contribution," or words to that effect. All they are really doing is appearing weak, leaving the choice to their prospective employer.

As I'll explain in Chapter Four, this is wrong. But, for now, it's important to know that you must decide what you want to do, focusing your accomplishments toward this single target.

How to Do Market Research

Your first task is to thoroughly research the potential market. You may wonder where you'll get this information. There are many different sources. You should use all of them to learn everything you can about your potential market, right from the start. Here are seven good sources.

Contacting Professionals

One way of getting market information is to call managers or friends at different companies. You will never be in a better position to do this than when you are a student. A student can frequently get through to top managers of companies, whereas people already employed have much more difficulty.

Some of my students have spoken to presidents and vice presidents of major corporations with just one phone call. Generally, this is because managers want to encourage future professionals interested in their field.

Call the manager of a company in your area of interest and say that you are a student thinking about a career in his or her profession. Add that you are not looking for a job right now, but that you would like to learn more about the work that he or she does. Many managers are willing to spend time helping you or they will assign someone to give you additional information. You could even be invited in for a visit.

The same is true of friends who have gone to work in your area of interest. Never be afraid of calling them to get information. If several turn you down, don't despair. Keep calling until you get the information you need.

Reading About the Industry

Of course, reading all you can about your line of interest will keep you on top of things. It will also give information about companies' products and problems, as well as information about opportunities in the field.

Even if you are not a business student, you should be familiar with such publications as the *Wall Street Journal, Fortune, Business Week,* and other business magazines or trade magazines that cover each industry in detail.

Plastics, aerospace, printing, and so on, all have their own trade magazines. If you are uncertain what magazines may be available, ask the managers in these industries what magazines they read. You can also visit a library and ask for the librarian to help locate magazines read by professionals in the area of business in which you're interested.

Attending Trade Shows

Another great source of information is trade shows. Trade shows are large exhibitions with all sorts of products, services, and presentations, pertaining to a particular industry. You can generally locate trade shows once you locate the industry's magazines. Many magazines publish a list of upcoming shows by geographical area. You can meet representatives from many companies that have booths and are displaying products. You can easily gather product information, information about companies, and lots more. You can also make valuable contacts. There's no other way to gather more information about a single industry in a single day.

Developing Relationships With Professors

Your professors may be great sources of information, especially if they are doing research in the areas in which you're interested or are industry consultants. Who better to discuss marketing with, for example, than a marketing professor who currently consults in marketing for a variety of companies. It's certainly worthwhile to develop friendships or relationships with professors with whom you have studied. Although their primary responsibility is to teach you, many professors may be willing to help if they know that you are really interested in the subject they are teaching. Of course, they may also be of value for business contacts later in your campaign.

University- and Association-Sponsored Lectures

Many schools and universities invite practicing professionals to give talks to students on various subjects, such as finance, marketing, and accounting. You can learn a great deal at these talks about the businesses the speakers are engaged in, and also about their jobs and companies. Again, you can also make contacts as well as ask questions. Talks are also given by a variety of professional organizations. You may be interested in joining such an organization, even if you are not a business student.

For example, the American Marketing Association has student divisions, as do management, finance, accounting, and other business associations. These groups are located right at your school. They will assist in career decisions, and provide contacts and motivations. Frequently, you may be eligible to join these associations even if you are not a business student. If you are planning to eventually enter into a particular business, these clubs and societies sponsor talks that can be of tremendous importance.

Working in Different Industries

As discussed in Chapter One, part-time jobs are a source of contacts, but they're also a source of valuable market research information. By working part time, you may also discover an industry that you really like—or really don't like; either way, it's a bonus. Even if you are working for little or no compensation, you'll definitely gain knowledge and market insight for your later job campaign.

Identifying Prospective Employers

Finally, you should research your potential market by identifying prospective employers by name. And I don't mean only the name of the company, but also the name of the manager you would potentially report to. Once you decide on the job you want, the geographical location, and the size of the company, you can consult directories that list the names, addresses, and telephone numbers of executives by job title. You can also use the telephone book.

Prospective bosses are easy to identify. Just think who the holder of the job you want would report to. If you want a job as an accountant, who does an accountant report to? Look for a title such as controller, vice president of accounting, or vice president of finance. If you are seeking a job in personnel, who would your boss be but the personnel manager, employment manager, or manager of human resources? An assistant product manager must report to a product manager, and so forth.

Let's say that you are interested in a job in planning. Simply go to the telephone book and pick a number of companies that you may be interested in working for. Naturally a company that employs planners must be fairly large. Next, call the company. When the receptionist answers, ask for the director of planning, or the vice president of planning. She may give you the direct number at the same time. If so, write it down. If she does not, she will connect you with the individual's secretary. Ask the secretary the name of the director or vice president of planning. This is who you would report to if you want to be a planner or work in planning. Then, ask to speak to the executive. Once you get the right person on the line, introduce yourself and call him or her by name. Say that, while you're not seeking a job as a planner at the present time, you're finishing your degree and would like to know more about planning as a potential career. Perhaps he or she would be willing to spend a little time with you, so that you can learn more about planning and how to start a career.

Market Segmentation

Your *customers*–the prospective employers who may be interested in hiring you–are not all the same. There are size differences in various industries in many geographical locations. They don't think alike or act alike. They don't all pay the same salaries, nor do they offer identical fringe benefits.

They have different philosophies of management and will respond differently to actions you take during your job-finding campaign. Since you cannot be everything to everybody, it is important to segment your potential market of employers. By doing so, you will you find the market segment with the right combination of factors that will make you the happiest, You will also be able to concentrate your resources, time, and effort toward specific firms where your background, experience, and individuality will be most desired.

Product Differentiation

> ***You must differentiate your experience, capabilities, and overall qualifications from other job seekers who are applying for your superior job.***

After you have defined your market and segmented it by job title, the size of the company, industry, geographical area, and so forth, you are ready to begin the process of product differentiation. That is:

To do this, go back to your resume. Look over the list of accomplishments for those that are well thought out. Choose those accomplishments that compliment the superior job you want. To do this, think about the accomplishments that are relevant to the job and that clearly indicate your superiority over any competition.

Let's say you have decided that you want to be a salesperson. Select accomplishments that have to do with selling that persuade people to do things, or that demonstrate your abilities through accomplishments of related tasks.

If you want to be a management trainee, look for your accomplishments that show leadership, maybe as an officer in a college organization, or as a part-time or temporary supervisor of others, or as a project manager.

If you want to be a researcher of one sort or another, look for resume accomplishments that show quantitative talents and the ability to analyze, make calculations, do face-to-face interviews, or organize research projects.

It is important that your accomplishments fit your superior job. Sometimes you will find spectacular accomplishments, but if they don't fit the superior job you have decided upon, don't use them.

Maybe you are seeking a position as an athletic coach at a school, and you speak five languages fluently. Should you list your language skills in support of a position as an athletic coach? The answer is no, unless the job requires that you speak one of the languages. If you're not required to instruct in one or more of these five languages, they are irrelevant to your duties. The prospective employer might even think that you are primarily a linguist who could not get a job in your own profession.

The same principle holds if you want to work in some other field. If you are looking for a job in engineering and have done great things in sales as a student, the sales job is probably irrelevant to the engineering job. Therefore, do not list it as one of your accomplishments–unless of course it is a sales engineer. Use of unrelated accomplishments can make you seem like a weaker candidate.

Remember that employers in any industry, whether business, government, or a nonprofit institution, are interested in the money you can make for the firm, how efficiently you can operate, and what you can accomplish. If you have done something in an entirely different area, including it in your sales letter will raise questions about your *real* interests and detract from your strengths. Others may do this, and they will appear to be a "jack-of-all-trades and master of none." But, having geared accomplishments toward a single goal, you will be identified as a superior candidate for the job you have selected.

This technique, based on a combination of market research, market segmentation, and product differentiation, helps to concentrate your resources and is one of the most important components of a successful job campaign. Using it, you will appear stronger than your competitors. You will demonstrate to your employer, even before you are hired, a commitment to your goal, backed by outstanding accomplishments. Marketers, using this technique, sell billions of dollars worth of products every year. Remember this lesson.

By concentrating your resources and focusing them on the target market you have developed, you can succeed in achieving a higher salary and a superior position.

Having geared your accomplishments
toward a single goal,
you will be identified as a superior candidate
for the job you have selected.

4 FOUR

Self-Advertising

Self-advertising is an extremely powerful tool that can be used during your campaign for a superior job.

This is true for three basic reasons:

- One, advertising exerts a tremendous influence on prospective buyers of a product or service. For this reason, many advertisers spend enormous amounts of money to get their message to prospective customers.
- Two, advertising allows you to reach more customers with your product. Of course, the product we're speaking of is you. With advertising you can reach and influence prospective employers who are seeking an individual with your background.
- And three, you control the message. Self-advertising allows you to build a favorable image of yourself in the mind of your prospective employer. Contrast this with an interview staged through your school, in which you present yourself and are asked questions by a company representative. You have far less control in this situation and a less-than-ideal opportunity to influence an employer.

Self-Advertising Usually Doesn't Work

After having noted the benefits of self-advertising, I must tell you that self-advertising usually does not work for job seekers. That's because most job seekers don't do it the right way. Every product is different and requires special advertising methods. Most job seekers select the least effective method. In fact, most elect to advertise in a classified section of a magazine or newspaper with the heading "Situations" or "Jobs Wanted."

This rarely works. Few employers actually read the job-wanted advertisements to fill their available positions. After all, they have a particular individual in mind, especially for a superior job. Why should they read these generalized advertisements on the off chance that someone might be available?

Also, job-wanted ads don't provide enough information to make a sale, which means that the advertiser won't get an interview. Joe Karbo, the famous mail-order man who sold more than one million copies of his book, *The Lazy Man's Way to Riches*, sold his product for only ten dollars. In order to do this, he took out a full-page newspaper advertisement that contained thousands of words and cost thousands of dollars.

Why should an employer buy your "product" based on a few words, when there are so many other "products" around? Finally, a job-wanted advertisement presents a poor image. It tells the prospective employer that the person is desperate and cannot get a job through the usual channels. Occasionally job-wanted advertising is effective, but it is difficult to make it work; and there is a better way to self-advertise. This other method is more powerful, and it works 100 percent of the time.

The Method of Self-Advertising That Works 100 Percent of the Time

Yes, there really is a method of self-advertising that works every single time, if done properly. This method is a direct-mail campaign in which you send sales letters directly to the people with the authority to hire and to make you an offer of a superior job.

This mailing is not just a bunch of printed letters sent at random to companies. Each letter is personalized by the name of the hiring person. The letter never goes to the personnel department. Remember that the personnel department never has the authority to hire you, only to stop you from being hired by screening you out. Also, the average personnel or employment manager rarely knows of superior jobs until some time after they become available.

I want to emphasize that I am not talking about sending a resume with a cover letter. You will never send a single resume. I will explain why shortly.

The secret is to write a sales letter so compelling that your potential employer cannot put it down and would be a fool not to give you an interview. You may wonder how in the world you can write such a powerful letter. Well, hold on, because I will show you this as well.

A direct-mail campaign to individuals with hiring authority results in quality interviews–not just interviews you may get by knowing a friend or a professor; not interviews that you receive as a result of interviewing with a number of companies through your school's career-development center; and not interviews you get after you've sent your resume to various personnel departments.

The sort of interview that results from a direct-mail campaign is one in which you are invited to meet your prospective boss as a job candidate. Your potential employer is already impressed with you and your qualifications as a result of your letter, and he or she has a specific job in mind. You're not just being interviewed on the off chance that he or she can make an opening for you because you are sharp or because he or she is impressed.

It is very important to know that this person *does* have the authority to make the hiring decision. Usually, if you have a favorable interview with the person to whom you sent your sales letter, you need to see and impress no one else. Meeting this individual alone is usually sufficient. Because you have already stated in your letter the exact position you want, when you receive the invitation for an interview, it is as a job candidate for *your* superior job.

Do you realize that, when you interview with all the companies at the school career-development center, you are competing with all the students at your school, and with hundreds–if not thousands– of students at other schools who are also graduating? Clearly, no company can hire hundreds or thousands of students. The numbers hired are small when compared to the numbers interviewed. It is not an overstatement to say that you have lots of competition.

Eliminating the competition is clearly a very important factor in being hired for the superior job you want.

When you write a direct-mail sales letter targeted at the superior job you want, you have very little competition if any at all.

Write a Dynamic, Self-Promoting Sales Letter

I previously stated that you would be able to write a letter so compelling that your future boss would have to be a fool not to invite you in for an interview. I have developed a formula to help you write this letter. You might even call it a *secret* formula. If you follow this formula, you will write a strong letter that will result in a number of quality interviews. The interviews, in turn, will result in superior job offers.

What is this secret formula? The acronym HOBBY. Each letter of the acronym represents a part of the formula: "H" for

Headline, "O" for Objective, the first "B" for Benefits, the second "B" for Believability, and "Y" for Yield.

Let's look at each part of this formula and see how you will write this powerful sales letter.

My Secret-Formula Sales Letter

H Headline
O Objective
B Benefits
B Believability
Y Yield

The Headline: An Attention Getter

The purpose of the first line of your letter is to grab the attention of your reader, the prospective employer. It should not be capitalized like a headline, but the effect should be the same. Select your most outstanding accomplishment from the list you developed in Chapter Two. This should be the strongest accomplishment that supports your candidacy for the superior job you want. Don't simply scribble down a line and let that stand. Spend some time working on your headline, cutting down the words, and increasing its impact.

The first time I used this method, I was an engineer who had been a department manager; I was seeking increased responsibilities as a manager of research and development. My headline read as follows:

I doubled the work output of my department while cutting engineering hours by 25 percent.

The positions I wanted would report to the vice president of engineering of a large company, or the president of a smaller, medium-sized company. Can you imagine a prospective boss, responsible for the engineering department, throwing away such a letter without reading further? Impossible? Well, that's precisely the result you are seeking.

For example, a journalism major who clearly wanted to be an associate editor wrote:

I was the editor of a college newspaper that won 5 famous journalism awards in 2 years.

An engineer who wanted a job as a designer wrote:

As a student, I designed a $1.98 control device in 2 months that has the potential to make $1 million a year in sales.

And a language major who wanted to work as a translator wrote:

Over a 3-year period, I translated more than 1 million words from English to German and from German to English while working part-time.

Note that, in all cases, the writers used short sentences that highlighted a single accomplishment in support of their specific job goal. Also note that the job candidates used figures instead of spelled-out numbers to give their accomplishment greater visual impact. In each case, the prospective employer who receives this letter will be forced to read on. An employer would have to be crazy to throw away such a letter without reading the next paragraph.

The Objective

The second letter in the magic formula word HOBBY is "O," which stands for *objective*. Your objective tells your prospective boss why you are writing. I like to get right to the point and say something like this:

I am writing in case you need a ___________. If you have an opening, or anticipate that one will be available soon, here are some other accomplishments that may interest you.

A short statement like this tells your potential boss exactly what you want. It sets you apart as someone who knows what he or she wants and has the self-confidence and fortitude to come right out and say it.

Sometimes, if your headline is outstanding and you have stated your objective, your prospective boss will continue to read even though he has no job at the present time. This phenomenon answers a question that I sometimes get from job seekers: "Doesn't stating an objective limit my options? Shouldn't I say that I am willing to take any job where my skills can be used for the major benefit of the company and so forth?" The answer is no. All employers realize such claims are nonsense. Every job seeker says something like this, and the employer feels that your real desires and interests are being concealed simply to get a job.

Also, when you leave things open, it puts the burden on the employer. He or she must stop and think what position might be open for such a person. Usually, even an executive will take the easy way out and simply send the letter to the employment department. Those who work in personnel will usually go no farther than checking your letter against a short list of current job openings. They will then send you a nice letter that tactfully indicates that, while you have outstanding qualifications, no jobs are currently open.

Let me tell you a little story about what once happened to me when I was seeking a position. It is typical of what happens to many job seekers, be they students or executives.

The situation was this: I had left my position as a senior research and development manager to go into executive recruiting. I then wished to return to the aerospace industry to work in marketing for a large company. I was very specific about what I wanted to be and where I wanted to go.

While researching what level position I should seek, I found that I wanted to become vice president of a major aerospace company. The chances of my getting such a position were slim because this industry usually tends to groom its top managers and promote from within.

On the other hand, I didn't rule out a vice presidency completely. I wrote two separate letters that listed different job objectives. One letter went to the presidents of major aerospace companies. It indicated my objective as vice president of marketing. The other letter was sent to the vice presidents of marketing of the same companies. It was identical to the first, except that it indicated that my objective was to be a marketing manager.

Picture this for a moment. I had written the same letter to the top executive of the company and to the individual with marketing responsibilities who reported to him or her. This shows, among other things, just how much you can do in finding superior jobs if you are willing to stick your neck out. But, after all, what would happen if the two did meet and converse about the two separate letters? At worst, they would know that I had high aspirations.

I received an invitation from the vice president of marketing in a division of a major aerospace company to come in for an interview. The interview went extremely well; during an almost full-day visit, I met other senior managers in the company, including vice presidents and the executive vice president. The only person I did not meet was the president of the company, who I learned was on an extended vacation and would not return for several weeks. Before the interview was over, the vice president of marketing said, "Bill, we really like your style, and you can expect an offer from us in the next few weeks."

When I returned home in the late afternoon, my wife greeted me with a letter from the personnel department of the same company. "I thought you had an interview with this company today," she said. "I did," I answered, "and I'm going to get a job offer from it." "Well then, what does this mean?" she asked as she handed me the letter.

When I saw the letter, I started laughing. The personnel department had written it in response to the one I had written to the president of the company. I was informed that there were no job openings currently available, but that they would keep my resume on file.

Of course, the president had never received the letter. As the president was gone for an extended period, the secretary had screened his mail. She had read my letter, realized what it was, and sent it to the personnel department. They responded with one of their standard form letters, so standard that they did not even stop to notice that I had never sent a resume, only a letter. A week later I received a job offer as marketing manager, despite the fact that, according to the personnel department, no openings existed.

Every now and then, a person will be so impressed with your letter that you will be offered another position, even though it was not stated as part of your objective. If this happens, you should consider the offer on the merits of the job. For example, I once was seeking a position as a research and development manager and was asked if I would fly to another city for an interview as a marketing manager. I had indicated no interest in such a job and had listed no qualifications for the job.

If this happens to you, you can always consider whether the job is a *superior job* by your criteria. But never, never leave it open, implying that the employer is supposed to make a decision for you. In marketing language, you will have failed to position yourself properly against your competition.

If you pick a clean, clear-cut objective and back it up with your resources (your accomplishments), I promise that you will be perceived as knowing what you are doing and where you want to go and possessing the necessary qualifications to get there.

You will get more interviews–and interviews of far better quality–than your classmates who go the old route of sending a resume with a cover letter and a career objective that reads, in effect, "I am willing to do anything that helps the company in whatever way my qualifications allow."

The Benefits

The first "B" in our formula, HOBBY, stands for *benefits*. One of the first things a neophyte copywriter is taught is that he or she should talk about benefits and not about attributes. For example, consider a person buying a drill. Unless this person is technically inclined, he or she really isn't interested in the fact that it has a high-impact case, is fire resistant, is so many inches long, weighs so many ounces, or is made of nickel-plated steel. What a person buying a drill really wants to know is its ability to make holes. After all, that's why a person wants to buy a drill. Right? The hole is the benefit.

In the same fashion, sophisticated marketers of cosmetics and cologne have discovered that they are not selling smell as much as they are selling romance and the ability to attract the opposite sex. Or, put another way, McDonald's is selling sizzle and aroma, not a piece of meat.

In the same way, you have to sell your benefits and not your attributes. So turn once again to your list of accomplishments and select four, five, or six of the strongest ones. They must support the objective that was stated in the previous paragraph of your letter. Work on each accomplishment so that it reads as if it were an individual headline. The following are a few good examples for various types of jobs.

Working part-time, I sold an average of $16,000 worth of women's shoes each month.

As a bank money-transfer clerk, I transferred $12 million daily via telephone CRT and teletype machines.

I represented 2,500 dormitory residents in negotiations with university officials.

I organized, managed, and motivated 126 people to sell 18,000 tickets for a fund-raiser that grossed $117,000.

I analyzed 23 different marketing situations and identified the central problem, analyzed alternative solutions, and developed recommendations for each company.

Note again that your accomplishments can be from a part-time job, a full-time job, work at school, or work and tasks done as a part of your academic courses. All of them count, provided they are important to a prospective employer.

As a sales manager, wouldn't you prefer to have someone working for you that had already organized, managed, and motivated 126 people to sell 18,000 Disneyland tickets for a

$117,000 fund-raiser? You would probably prefer such a job candidate over someone who had experience as a salesperson but couldn't quantify it and say or show what he or she had actually done–that's the difference between a real benefit and just a lot of talk.

Note how compelling these sentences are. They are short, and they sell you as a strong candidate. They sell your benefits through quantitative examples, not through adjectives.

You may say, "Well, gee, I know I've done a lot of things; for example, I conducted a lot of interviews." Well, you shouldn't just say "a lot" of interviews. You must always say that you conducted 981 interviews, 43 interviews, or whatever "a lot" happens to be. Furthermore, don't say you did "a good job." It's necessary to show quantitatively exactly what kind of job you did.

Describe the job you did in terms that sell your performance: percentages and dollars and figures.

Remember that short, to-the-point sentences with figures sell. If you don't have the figures readily available, sit down, think back, and estimate. Give the best and most accurate estimate that you can. But when you make your estimate, state it unconditionally. Don't say "about" or "approximately"–this only weakens your accomplishment. A little hint: If you are estimating, it's better to estimate an odd number rather than an even one. Psychologically, the odd number is more credible. If you happen to know the exact figure, of course, and it comes out even, so be it.

Believability

The second "B" in HOBBY stands for *believability.* The person who reads your compelling sales letter must be impressed with your accomplishments. But there is no proof of them. It's only your word. So we must devise some way to build and ensure the letter's believability. You do so by stating something that can easily be confirmed by a letter or phone call, such as the date you received or expect to receive your degree from your college or university. When you include this information, your entire letter appears more believable.

If you have already graduated, I would simply say:

"I graduated from ________ University with a degree in __________."

Many recent graduates and students ask if they should state the year they graduated. If your objective matches your age, I would state the year. If you are too young for your job objective or, in rare cases, too old for your job objective, I would omit it. The reason, of course, is that in most cases the year you graduated from college gives away your age.

What if you have not yet graduated at the time that you conduct your direct-mail campaign? You can say something like this:

"I will be graduating this June from ________ University with a degree."

Should you state your type of degree? If your degree supports the job objective, spell it out and state exactly what type of degree you have. On the other hand, if your degree in no way– or only remotely–supports your job objective, it is best to omit it. For example, if you have a Bachelor of Arts degree in, say, ancient history, and your job objective is stock-market analyst, then I would omit the actual title of the degree and state only that you have a B.A. degree.

On the other hand, if your B.A. in ancient history supports your superior job objective, then do not omit it. This concept holds true for every discipline and for every different type of degree that one may have.

Yield

The last letter in HOBBY is "Y," which stands for *yield.* One definition of yield is *to submit to urging or persuasion.* This is what you have done in your sales letter. You have persuaded your prospective boss and, at this point, you wish for him or her to yield by acting. Make it very clear what action you want your prospective boss to take.

In your last paragraph, write something like this:

I would be pleased to discuss additional details of my background and experience in a personal interview.

It's just that simple. This short sentence is the final part of your letter that will persuade your prospective boss to yield and act in the way you wish.

Finally, close your letter with *Sincerely* and sign each individually, even though your basic letter will be mass produced to save time and expense.

Over the years I have found that most invitations for interviews are issued by telephone. This is because you are not dealing with someone who can screen you out and stop you from getting the job. You are dealing with the one who has the authority to hire you, the manager to whom you will report. Managers tend to be action oriented; instead of writing, they are more likely to telephone soon after reading your letter.

Naturally, this is in your best interest. The sooner your prospective boss acts, the more likely it is that he or she will hire you. To encourage a quick response, type your telephone number on the opposite side of the paper from your signature. Then it is easy for the executive to locate. You have stated that you are willing to come in for an interview and have implied that you expect to be invited. Your telephone number, placed at the end of the letter, makes it very easy to call at once.

I know you may be busy with classes, a job, or something else that might prevent you from monitoring a telephone. However, you have several alternatives. One is to have a friend or relative answer the phone. The name and telephone number of a caller can be taken so that the call can be returned as soon as possible. A dorm phone is not very helpful or professional for this purpose; if you can't have someone take messages, you should seek another solution.

An alternative is to hire an answering service while you are job hunting. A campaign such as the one described here should not take very long. Therefore, you should not have to pay a great deal of money for the service. My only word of caution about answering services is to be sure that you are getting good service.

Unfortunately, some answering services use inexperienced operators. They often are rude, put people on hold for long periods, or otherwise may annoy any professional who happens to call. If you engage an answering service, check on them occasionally by dialing the number yourself. You don't want to lose any high-quality interviews because of a poor telephone receptionist.

Another solution is available if you have a private phone but cannot always answer. An answering machine is quite acceptable. Just be sure you make a professional-sounding tape, requesting that the caller leave his or her name, a company name, and telephone number. You may also state that you are currently in class and will return the call as soon as possible

If none of these solutions is right for you, state in your letter the hours you are available. The best place is beside the telephone number. There are two limitations to doing this however. First, you must always be available during the hours you have stated. Second, the times you have written may be several hours away, forcing your prospective employer to wait. Remember that the number of interviews you get from your mailing will decrease over a short period of time.

You will maximize the number of interviews if your prospective employers can reach you instantly.

It is very important to word your sales letter as I have shown you, following the outline of the word HOBBY. This will help you to create a more powerful sales letter than you ever believed possible. Some sample sales letters, written by my students, are included in Chapter Five.

How to Personalize Every Letter

When you write your letters, it's very important to use the correct title and the exact name of the person who occupies the position to which you would report. To do this, it's necessary to be able to get these names in large quantities. Don't worry, it's a lot easier than you may think. There are many directories available that list executives' names and positions. Here are a few:

Dun and Bradstreet's Million-Dollar Directory lists executives of 120,000 firms worth more than $500,000 with the top 45,000 firms listed in order of net worth.

Standard and Poor's Register of Corporations, Directors and Executives contains the names of 400,000 executives from 38,000 companies.

Standard Directory of Advertisers lists 80,000 executives from 17,000 companies advertising nationally.

Thomas Register of American Manufacturers lists 100,000 manufacturers by product and location.

There are also directories available that list companies and executives for most major industries, such as plastic, steel, and so on. For instance, *World Aviation Directory* lists directories and companies in the aerospace industry. Most of these directories can be found in your university library.

Other sources of important information are published locally by city or state Chambers of Commerce. Not only are companies listed and described, but these directories also provide the addresses and names of many executives.

Yet another source of names are list brokers. List brokers rent and sell lists of executives by function, geographical area, industry, and level. The lists rent for $60 to $70 per thousand. Check the yellow pages in your phone book for the names of list brokers in your area.

Do not overlook this step. It is very important that your letter includes the executive's name as well as his or her title.

It's also very important to make certain that your sales letter does not look anything like a resume. If it does, it will be discovered, screened out by the secretary, and sent directly to the personnel department. You will then receive one of their form letters telling you how wonderful your resume (which you didn't send) is.

One way both of avoiding this and impressing your prospective boss is to use the best-looking letter possible.

The best color choices for paper are plain white or slightly off-white, and you should buy the finest-quality paper you can afford.

Your address should be printed at the top of the letter. I like to have this done using the thermograph process. This process raises the letters as though they were engraved. These letters will represent you to your prospective employers and will help get your letter past the secretary.

Now you may wonder how you will be able to type a large number of letters and still have time to do anything else. Take a plain sheet of paper the exact size of the stationery you purchased. Type the body of your letter on this plain sheet of paper, providing space for the address heading as well as the date and salutation, which will be typed later. This becomes the "camera-ready" copy that you take to your printer. The printer will use this master to make a plate to print your sales letter on your stationery with the preprinted heading.

Once this step is complete, you are in a position to personalize each letter, using the same typewriter that was used to type the body of the letter so that the typeface matches. When you insert the paper into the typewriter to type the date, executive's name, address, and salutation, be careful to align the margins and lines. This preprinted method can be detected because the ink color will differ slightly from the typewriter ribbon. However, it is far cheaper to create your sales letters this way than to have each typed individually. Obviously, if you have a computer and associated printer, you can easily customize your letters.

Again, even though the body of your letter has been printed, each letter must be individually signed by you. I like to use blue ink, so that it stands out against the black ink of the printing and the typewriter.

How Many Letters Should You Send?

I know you are wondering how many letters to send as well as what results you can expect. I wish that I could give you a firm answer, but the answer varies widely depending on many factors, including economic conditions, the demand for the type of job you want, the level of the job, in addition to the quality of your sales letter.

Normally I have found that a two- to three-percent response can be expected. Of the letters you send, two to three percent of the people will invite you for an interview. Now that may not sound like very many, but we're talking about quality interviews in which you are a candidate for the specific job you want and for which you will have very little competition. Also, the number of interviews can be increased significantly if you send a larger number of letters. I recommend that you mail 1,000 letters, if possible. This might sound like a lot, but it ensures that you'll have the greatest success possible for an interview and a very good chance of landing a truly superior job.

Consider the following: If you send only 100 letters, you will get two to three quality interviews. This response rate has two disadvantages:

- First, you will not get enough experience in interviewing. Unless you are very unusual, you need practice in this; and the more interviews that you are able to get, the better.

Frankly, you may blow a couple at first as you learn how to present yourself effectively.

- Second, to get a large number of offers, you need to go on a large number of interviews. Having multiple options puts you in charge of the situation, ensuring that you get the best job possible. So, rather than sending just 100 and planning on 2 or 3 interviews, send 1,000. It may cost a little more in money and time, but it will be well worth it.

Is there any possibility of sending fewer letters and having great success? Well, frankly, yes, it is possible. One of my students sent only 39 letters yet had so many invitations for interviews that he had to start turning them down, as he could not keep up with the demand. This does happen. However, why not expect the best but be prepared for the worst? If you send 1000 letters, and if you do it right, the results will make life interesting: 20 to 30 quality interviews with a high probability of getting a number of offers for superior jobs.

This Is a Sales Letter, Not a Cover Letter

I want to emphasize that the letter we discussed in this chapter is *not* a cover letter. A few students feel a little nervous about sending a letter without a resume. After all, they have been taught that the only way to get an interview, and a job, is with a resume.

Now I am saying that this is not so. I must tell you this right now: If you use the sales letter and enclose a resume, it will not work. You will not get the return I promised, and you will not get the quality interviews that are necessary for you to get a superior job. So please don't do this.

This really puts you in the driver's seat, allowing you to negotiate for a number of superior jobs.

Follow all of the directions exactly as outlined in this book and I promise you will be amazed at the results.

What to Do if You Get Poor Results

For various reasons, you may receive poor results with the first mailing. If this happens, don't be discouraged.

First, you should recheck each step we've discussed. Did you use high-quality stationery and have it printed as I indicated? Is each letter personalized with the name of your prospective employer, as well as his or her job title? Did you sign each letter individually? Is the letter written exactly as the HOBBY formula outlines? Are all your accomplishments quantified numerically? Is your telephone number visible on the letter? Do you have a telephone that's being watched all day? If you have already done these things, then take the following steps.

1. Chapter Five consists of examples of successful letters written by students. Using your list of accomplishments that you developed in Chapter Two, make certain that your letter presents them well. Sometimes a very small change will make a big difference in results. One sales letter may result in only a few invitations for an interview, but a small change in the letter may double the number of invitations that you receive.

2. If you don't receive favorable responses after a few weeks, follow up your letters with telephone calls. To avoid being screened out by the secretary, call before 8:00 a.m. or after 5:00 p.m. In many cases the executive will be working, but the secretary probably won't. If the secretary can't be avoided, you may have some problem in getting through. If the secretary asks the subject of your call, you can say it's a private matter regarding a personal letter you wrote. State no more. If you explain that it has to do with a job, rest assured that the secretary will refer you to the employment department.

There are no competitors, and there is little chance that anyone can screen you out of the job.

If the secretary insists on knowing why you are calling, state that it has to do with personal business and to please let the executive know that you called. Then leave your number with a cordial "Thank you."

3. Make changes in your letter and mail it to the same executives again. Business conditions change rapidly; one week a company may not respond to your letter, but three weeks later you may get an immediate, eager response. The simple reason may be that while the letter was impressive, no job was available. Three weeks later, however, such a job could be open.

4. Expand your mailing to include additional managers and executives. There will be some extra names if your initial mailing didn't use the entire list; or, if you decide to extend your search to other geographical areas or industries, you can easily increase your mailing to include additional executives.

Why the Sales-Letter Approach Works

The sales-letter approach works because of the business environment. Unlike the situation in which you are meeting company representatives at the school's career-development center, the sales letter puts you in touch with the executive who is doing the hiring. Frequently the employment department doesn't even know that a superior job exists or that there is any opening at all.

You stand out immediately as a self-sufficient individual who is ready to accept responsibility for the job you have requested.

Frequently, when I have used this method, I have received an immediate call from an executive who sounded almost desperate. He would say, "Our vice president of marketing resigned only yesterday evening. When I came to work this morning I didn't know what we were going to do. And before contacting anyone I received and read your letter. It was almost as if fate was bringing us together." Amazingly, sometimes in a single mailing, I would get the same response from several different companies. Fate was looking out for everyone!

This is very important. Only when you're using the sales letter approach can your letter go into a situation where *you* are needed—your particular qualifications and your particular accomplishments as a specialist for the superior job.

You appear to be very qualified for the job you want.

Your sales letter can fail in only two situations: One, you wrote a poor sales letter, failing to focus on a specific objective, or you did something other than what was specified in the preceding chapters; or two, there wasn't an available position of the type you wanted in any of the companies that you contacted.

Can Your Letter Be Sent While You Negotiate Through Normal Channels?

Sometimes I am told by students that they have already made contact through the normal channels—through a friend, the human resources department, or perhaps the visiting manager at the career-development center. "Will a sales letter like this screw things up?" In my experience, your sales letter can only help—not hurt—your chances. After all, a company wants to hire you because of what you can do for it. An executive who is interested in hiring you after receiving your letter certainly isn't going to be uninterested when he or she knows that you have also met someone at the career-development center.

Along the same lines, why should someone be turned off simply because you have the smarts to write a terrific sales letter outlining the reasons that a company must have your services? They *won't* be turned off, and your sales letter can *only* help your chances for a job.

Whenever you're afraid of doing one of the techniques I have recommended, remember the result of my letters to the president and to the vice president of marketing in the same company, asking for jobs as a vice president of marketing and as a marketing manager. Believe me when I tell you that showing off your abilities can never hurt if a company thinks they can increase their profitability or efficiency by hiring you.

I consider this chapter one of the most important in this entire book. Through it you will obtain quality interviews, and a number of them will lead to offers for superior jobs. But it's up to you. Don't delay. You must start now on your own and begin the process. It's certainly more trouble than simply going down to the career-development center or than having your resume printed and doing things in the same old way. But it is certainly worth the trouble. Do you know that many companies will normally increase your salary only five percent a year or less? Yet you are probably worth far more to them. Thus, your initial salary is extremely important. It's also very difficult to advance in some companies, simply because so many executives have seniority. It may take much longer if you start at the bottom. Therefore, a week or so spent now in preparing this direct-mail campaign can be worth years to you in salary and advancement in any company. Take the time now and save years of ladder climbing later in your career!

A week or so spent preparing this direct-mail campaign can be worth years in salary and advancement in any company.

5

FIVE

Winning Sales Letters

Kathy A. Spelling
1071 Spice Lane
Columbia, Missouri 65211

August 16, 1999

Mr. A.B. Smith
Director of Marketing Research
Advantage Research, Inc.
571 Beck Street
St. Louis, Missouri 65207

Dear Mr. Smith:

I averaged 45 face-to-face interviews per week for the United States Census Bureau.

I am writing to you in case you are looking for someone as an assistant marketing researcher. If so, I have also:

> Conducted 128 telephone interviews.
>
> Designed, pretested, and revised a 40-item questionnaire used for a consumer demand study that resulted in 520 responses out of 1,000.
>
> Compiled, tabulated, and performed statistical analysis on data gathered from the field in 3 major studies.
>
> Achieved a 97 percent success rate in obtaining answers to sensitive questions.
>
> Designed, conducted, and analyzed the final results of a $14,000 unobtrusive observational survey.

I will receive a Bachelor of Science degree in marketing from the University of Missouri, Columbia, in December.

I would like very much to have a face-to-face interview with you.

Sincerely,

Kathy A. Spelling
Telephone: (314) 555-4116

Allen C. Klein
107 George Avenue
Columbus, Ohio 43210

December 2, 1999

Mr. W.W. Burt
City Editor
New Day Times
1130 Hope Street
Los Angeles, California 90030

Dear Mr. Burt:

I covered and wrote 107 stories for high school and university papers.

I am writing in case you need a junior reporter for your newspaper. If you do, you may be interested in some other things I have done that are relevant:

- My story on university housing practices was picked up by a major newspaper with a circulation of over 300,000.
- I received the *Star Quill* award for being the top reporter for the university newspaper.
- While still a college sophomore, I succeeded in writing stories based on the interviews I conducted with the top 5 politicians in my state.
- As vice president of Ohio State University's Journalism Club, I recruited 21 national figures as guest speakers.

I will be graduating from Ohio State University at Columbus this month with a B.A. degree in journalism.

I would very much like to meet you face to face to discuss further the details of my background and experience. Please contact me at (614) 555-2897, 4:30 to 9:30 p.m. eastern standard time.

Sincerely,

Allen C. Klein

Janice E. Brown
955 Sycamore Street
Auburn, Alabama 36830

April 2, 1999

Mrs. Maria D. Cubbard
Principal
ABC Elementary School
Auburn, Alabama 36830

Dear Mrs. Cubbard:

I developed a new technique for teaching penmanship that has been adopted by 7 schools and is being taught to more than 3,000 students.

I am writing to you in case you need an elementary school teacher. If you do, you may be interested in other things I have done:

> As a teacher's aide, I assisted in teaching 6 different classes in 7 schools. I received ratings of good to outstanding from 9 supervising teachers and staff evaluators.
>
> While still in college, I wrote an article, "Teaching to Write Right," for elementary teachers.
>
> I successfully taught crafts and good citizenship to an average of 216 campers for 3 years at Camp Sam during the summers of 1990, '91, and '92.
>
> I received an award for the best presentation while teaching a communication class, fall 1991.

I will be completing my Bachelor of Arts degree in education at Auburn University in May.

Can we meet to further discuss the details of my experience and your needs?

Sincerely,

Janice E. Brown
(205) 555-1475

Karen I. Igato
757 Mountain Drive
Los Angeles, California 90023

May 10, 1999

Mr. Joseph Lu
President
Far East Import/Export
722 Light Street
Los Angeles, California 90009

Dear Mr. Lu:

I have acted as both a Chinese and a Japanese language interpreter for 7 different groups of foreign businessmen from 3 Asian countries.

I am writing in case you need an oriental language correspondent or interpreter. If you do, you may be interested in other things I have done along these lines:

- Graded fluent in Japanese, Mandarin, and Cantonese Chinese under U.S. State Department exams in reading, writing, and comprehension.
- Traveled extensively in 12 different countries in Asia and attended for one year a Japanese school in Tokyo, Japan.
- Have maintained correspondence in 2 dialects of Chinese and Japanese with 8 different correspondents.
- Worked one summer with the East Wind Trading Agency as an interpreter and correspondent. Translated 43 different letters and documents either from Japanese into English or from English into Japanese.

I will be completing my bachelor's degree in oriental languages from UCLA at the end of May.

I would like to meet you to discuss further the details about my background in a personal interview.

Sincerely yours,

Karen I. Igato
(213) 555-0724

William N. Town
22 Daytona Road
College Park, Maryland 20742

May 8, 1999

Dr. George N. Davis
Director
NYZ Developmental Labs
177 Bridgepark Road
Baltimore, Maryland 20740

Dear Dr. Davis:

I prepared a 276-page technical manual, as part of a government contract, in less than one month while working part-time.

I am writing to you in case you need a technical writer. If you do, you may be interested in other things I have done that are relevant to this position:

> Authored 3 technical articles based on interviews with experts in the areas represented.
>
> Developed and wrote advertising copy for 11 different technical products for major U.S. companies as part of a course in technical writing.
>
> Consulted with and assisted faculty of the University of Maryland in developing 7 different proposals for grants in technical areas.
>
> As a member of the Technical Writers Club, wrote copy, brochures, and posters that assisted in attracting 37 new members in a single semester.

I will be graduating with a B.A. degree in English literature from the University of Maryland this month.

I would like to meet you to discuss further the details of my qualifications and experience as a technical writer. You can reach me at (301) 555-8250.

Sincerely,

William N. Town

Robert K. Kirk
2107 N. Central Avenue
Denver, Colorado 80210

September 1, 1999

Mr. Wagner
Owner
TopNotch Cars
207 South Street
Denver, Colorado 80211

Dear. Mr. Wagner:

At Mike's Auto, I sold 921 used cars in 7 months.

I am writing to you in the hope that you might be interested in someone with my capabilities as a used car salesman. If you are, here are some other things I've done that might interest you:

> At Right Auto, I made $5,000 in commissions one summer selling tires, brakes, shocks, etc.
>
> At S.P. Motors, I was a sales associate and responsible for finding leads. I averaged 5 leads a day while working part-time for more than 8 months.
>
> At Huntington College, I coordinated a fund-raising drive for the Distributive Education Clubs of America that raised $9,400.

Currently, I am attending the University of Denver where I am majoring in finance. I am seeking a part-time position so I can continue my education. I would be happy to discuss my qualifications with you in a face-to-face interview.

Sincerely,

Robert K. Kirk
Telephone: (303) 555-3297

Gloria M. Williams
55 South Gray Avenue
Louisville, Kentucky 40208

February 9, 1999

Mr. John J. Blondes
Branch Sales Manager
ABC Company
1234 South Street
Louisville, Kentucky 40208

Dear. Mr. Blondes:

While working at a major department store, I exceeded my daily sales goal by an average of 50 percent.

I am writing to you in case you are in need of a sales representative. If you are, here are some of my other accomplishments that might interest you:

- At Oldening Industries, I helped successfully launch their first direct-mail campaign by personally contacting 2,117 companies. This doubled our mailing list.
- At Northern Products, I was responsible for finding jobs for 115 professional personnel after a major layoff. I placed 87 employees for a 76 percent success rate by personal contact.
- At Super Pine, I reduced the percentage of back orders by 16 percent in 4 weeks.

I will be graduating in June from the School of Business Administration at the University of Louisville with a degree in marketing.

I would very much like to meet you to discuss my background in more detail.

Sincerely,

Gloria M. Williams
(502) 555-7071

Barbara Barco
14216 Waterhouse Road
Urbana, Illinois 61801

August 30, 1999

Mr. Peter J. Smith
President
Oldtown Company
150 Universal Street
Chicago, Illinois 60611

Dear Mr. Smith:

While in a government agency, I controlled 95 percent of the department's projects with a staff of 125.

I am writing to learn if you need an administrative assistant. If you do, you may be interested in some of the other things I have done:

> As president of a professional management organization, with an allocated budget of $1,900, I planned, organized, and motivated other people to attain 30 members per quarter.
>
> As vice president administrator of a public relations committee, I successfully promoted yearly activities by making 17 personal presentations and by writing to 59 chief executives of major corporations.
>
> As a marketing student, I conducted 7 market research studies and consulted for a private firm.

I will graduate from the University of Illinois at Urbana-Champaign in September with a degree in marketing management.

I would be happy to meet you to discuss my background in greater detail.

Sincerely,

Barbara Barco
Telephone: (217) 555-4567

George D. Ross
527 Jackson Street
College Station, Texas 77843

May 2, 1999

Mr. Harry B. Prentice
President
Prentice Company
6789 3rd Street
Austin, Texas 77321

Dear Mr. Prentice:

I developed a revised hiring plan for a major automobile parts franchise that has the potential to decrease personnel turnover by 22 percent.

I am writing to learn if you need a personnel manager. If you do, you may be interested in some of the other things I have done:

> I was in charge of hiring for a small retail store with 12 employees. While similar stores were suffering a 25 to 35 percent turnover every year, my store lost only two employees in 3 years.
>
> I developed a profile of highly productive retail employees for a university course. This profile was successfully applied by 5 retailers in the local area who reported an average productivity increase of 9 percent.
>
> At an experimental management clinic, I organized and motivated 26 students to perform various tasks and received the top class grade of 98 percent.

I will receive my B.S. degree in management from Texas A&M in June.

I would be happy to meet you to discuss further the details of what I have done and how it may be applied to your business.

Sincerely,

George D. Ross
(409) 555-7607

Frank R. Jones
631 Orange Coast Street
Kansas City, Kansas 66800

May 15, 1999

Mr. Jack Green
President
Sunflower Art
5 Bright Street
Kansas City, Kansas 66800

Dear Mr. Green:

I received the dean's award for the best commercial art drawing of 1991.

I am writing to you in case you need a commercial artist. If you do, here are some other things I have accomplished that may interest you:

- Completed 9 line drawings for a new product introduced by General Motors.
- Served as head artist, University Times. Completed 23 pieces of artwork published by the University Times over a 2-year period.
- Freelanced for 2 different advertising agencies over a 3-year period. Successfully completed 12 different commercial art assignments.
- Did voluntary artwork for 4 student organizations including the development of concepts and drawings of 17 different pieces.
- Won first place in a university contest for drawing the best poster representing United Way.

I will be completing my B.A. degree in commercial art at Emporia State University this June.

I would like to meet you to discuss further the details of my qualifications as a commercial artist.

Sincerely yours,

Frank R. Jones
(913) 555-1681

Allen W. Cranwell
1218 Salt Avenue
Dayton, Ohio 45433

May 4, 1999

Mr. Alvin Carter
Manager, Administrative Department
Grate Way Construction Company
190 West Sixth Street
Dayton, Ohio 45435

Dear. Mr. Carter:

I ran a 280-unit, $10 million condominium project.

I am writing to you in case you are in need of a manager's assistant, budget control.

At a major construction company, I:

> Established a standard cost accounting system to control a $10 million project.
>
> Charted cash flow of $30,000 per month.
>
> Budgeted funds of $300,000 per year.
>
> Directed 5 subcontractors.
>
> Maintained liaison with 7 government officials.
>
> Dealt with 13 customers.
>
> Maintained bank and financial relationships.

I have a B.S. degree in civil engineering from California State University, Los Angeles, and will receive an MBA specializing in finance from Wright State University in June.

I would very much like to meet you so that we can discuss my background in more detail. I can be reached at (513) 555-5834 from 9:00 a.m. to 5:00 p.m.

Sincerely,

Allen W. Cranwell

MICHAEL GREEN
1704 Park Lane
Huntington, California 92059

December 7, 1999

Mr. William McLaughlin, Branch Sales Manager
ABC Company
1234 South Street
Los Angeles, CA 12345

Dear. Mr. McLaughlin:

While at Johnson's Business Machines, I reduced the time to qualify sales leads from 66 days to 7 days.

I am writing to you in case you are in need of an information processing salesman. If so, you may be interested in some of my other accomplishments.

At Johnson's Business Machines, I:

- Demonstrated equipment to prospective customers.
- Trained customers and their staffs on newly purchased equipment.

At USC, I:

- Organized, managed, and motivated 126 people to sell 18,000 Disneyland tickets for a fund-raiser that grossed $151,000.
- Represented 2,500 dorm residents to university officials.

In my present position, I:

- Sold $18,000 worth of contracts at $36 each in less than two months.
- Developed a proposal to initiate a direct mail campaign that was accepted by top management with estimated sales of $100,000.

I will be graduating this December from the School of Business Administration, University of Southern California, with a marketing management degree.

I would very much like to meet you so that we can discuss my background in more detail and review my qualifications to be a sales representative at ABC Company.

Sincerely,

Michael Green
(213) 555-2099

JEFFREY L. DAVIS
2054 Garvis
Alhambra, California 90803

March 24,1999

Ms. A. Matthias, President
ABC Store
155 Mission Avenue
Newport Beach, California 12345

Dear Ms. Matthias:

With an international advertising agency, I made 277 cold calls, tracked 83 leads, and conducted 18 personal interviews with small business owners for new account development.

I am writing because you may be in need of someone with my capabilities as a business manager. If you do, you may be interested in some of my other accomplishments:

> At Drakes Department Store: As a sales associate, I sold an average of $16,000 worth of women's shoes each month on a part-time basis. I also developed a stockroom management system that expedited locating merchandise. This system increased the efficiency and the productivity of each sales associate.
>
> At California State University, Los Angeles: As an administrative management assistant, I redesigned and implemented a survey for a $6 million campus housing project. This survey was successfully distributed to 2,600 students.
>
> In the U.S. Air Force: As a sergeant, I managed a support staff of 3 and controlled an inventory of $100,000 to $200,000 in aircraft parts per day. I also scheduled the work to be performed on 18 base aircraft.

I will have a B.S. degree in marketing from California State University, Los Angeles, in August.

I would like very much to meet you to discuss my background in more detail and review my qualifications.

Sincerely,

Jeffrey L. Davis
Telephone: (213) 555-2001

George A. Duer
10198 Fireside Drive
Racine, Wisconsin 53705

March 20, 1999

Mr. James Paule
Manager, Purchasing Department
Racine Technical Corporation
115 Buy Street
Racine, Wisconsin 53705

Dear Mr. Paule:

At PAC Import Company, I discovered and purchased a cube puzzle from a manufacturer in Hong Kong shortly after its introduction. As a result, PAC beat all local competition and earned $30,000 in profits.

I am writing to you in case you need a merchandise buyer. If so, you may be interested in some of my other accomplishments:

- As a part-time import buyer, I researched and recommended purchase of more than 13 successful import items resulting in sales of $297,000.
- I researched and developed a marketing plan for a retail business and planned the purchase of 5 new items with sales potential in excess of $90,000.
- I accomplished 3 major research studies on demographics and ethnic make-up of the Racine area.
- While a student, I managed a budget of $4,200 and acted as buying agent for the University of Wisconsin Drama Club.

I will be graduating from the University of Wisconsin in May with a B.A. degree in management.

I would very much like to meet you to discuss additional details of my qualifications.

Sincerely,

George A. Duer
Telephone: (414) 555-0686

Arthur P. Rey
4512 Glen Echo Drive
Pasadena, California 91107

June 1, 1999

Ms. W.A. Jones
President
All Day Shipping, Inc.
501 4th Avenue
Long Beach, California 90009

Dear Ms. Jones:

While at Go Fast Shipping, I developed the inbound traffic department and increased efficiency by 30 percent, saving $13,000 in overall department costs.

I am writing because you may be interested in my qualifications and background as a traffic manager:

> At Zip Trading Company, I developed a new bill of lading form that was adopted at all branch offices. Error rate was reduced an estimated 14 percent.
>
> At New Export, Inc., I reworked distribution plans and found a more efficient way of transporting our products that cut costs by 13 percent.
>
> While in the U.S. Navy, I was assigned to the supply department. I was commended for designing new transportation forms that increased overall efficiency and are saving the Navy $15,000 a year.

I will receive a B.S. degree in transportation from California State University, Los Angeles, in June.

I would be happy to meet with you to discuss my background and experience in more detail.

Sincerely,

Arthur P. Rey
(213) 555-1211

John P. Matkins
507 N. Aimes Street
Tempe, Arizona 85281

November 21, 1999

Ms. S. Tomkins
Forward Financial Corporation
2013 Handler Boulevard
Phoenix, Arizona 85350

Dear Ms. Tomkins:

While at 1st National Bank of Arizona, I increased new accounts development by $1 million in 2 days.

I am writing to learn if you need a senior lending officer. If so, you may be interested in some of my other accomplishments:

- At 1st National Bank, I redesigned the lending files system. The time required to locate information decreased 23 percent. I also developed $500,000 in new loans in a month.
- As membership chairman of the Economics Club at Arizona State University, I recruited 16 student members in one hour.
- Working full-time while attending the university, I expanded the lending department 11 percent, got 100 percent participation from our staff while in charge of the United Way campaign, and organized a get-acquainted party with top management and the branch VIP customers. This effort resulted in an increase of 34 percent in branch deposits.

I will be graduating this December from the School of Business Administration, Arizona State University, Tempe, with a B.A. degree in finance.

I would like to have the opportunity to meet at your convenience to discuss in detail my qualifications and possible future with your corporation. I can be reached at (201) 555-1336.

Sincerely,

John P. Matkins

Richard B. Mann
123 4th Avenue
Fayetteville, Arkansas 72701

July 9, 1999

Mr. Darryl B. Maddox
Coopers and Associates
54 Stevens Boulevard
Fayetteville, Arkansas 72701

Dear Mr. Maddox:

As a trouble-shooter in an accounting department, I increased output by 36 percent without loss of accuracy.

I am writing in case you are in need of an auditor. If you are, you may be interested in some of my other accomplishments:

- At Zeus Sales Company, I helped rebuild and assigned 14 general ledger accounts for the company's newly installed in-house computer. This saved the company an estimated 16 percent per year in time.
- At Lawson, Inc., I assisted independent auditors in preparing 21 audit working papers.
- At the same time, working in the payroll department, I maintained all records and prepared journal entries for 86 employees. I also assisted the assistant controller in rebuilding and assigning new general ledger accounts for the newly installed in-house computer and assisted in the conversion of manual bookkeeping to computers.
- At Universal Accounts, Inc., I managed the books of a company with a $20,500 inventory and $238,450 total assets, and I was responsible for the tax liability.
- At B and J Fashions, I processed 112 factory and administrative personnel every week.

I will be graduating in August from the School of Business Administration at the University of Arkansas with a Bachelor of Science degree in accounting.

I would like very much for us to meet to discuss my background in more detail.

Sincerely yours,

Richard B. Mann
(501) 555-5789

Nancy E. Block
147 Forest Drive
Philadelphia, Pennsylvania 19121

May 14, 1999

Mr. James Sparrow, President
Sparrow and Associates
157 Willow Way
Philadelphia, Pennsylvania 19122

Dear Mr. Sparrow:

I wrote advertising copy that resulted in 141 responses in one week.

I am writing in case you need an advertising copywriter. If you do, here are some other things that I have done:

> As part of an advertising course, I wrote copy for 17 full-page ads for 17 different products. I received an "A" evaluation for each one.
>
> I prepared 22 ads as a copywriter for a university newspaper for 7 different clients over a 2-year period. Every client requested additional advertising.
>
> I analyzed 51 different national ads by well-known copywriters and agencies. In every case I specified elements that worked and those that did not and correlated these with the actual results from the ads.
>
> I attended 5 seminars on copywriting at my own expense.

In June I will be graduating from Temple University with a B.A. degree in English.

My ambition is to be a full-time copywriter with your agency. I would very much like to meet you to discuss my experience and qualifications for this position.

Sincerely,

Nancy E. Block
Telephone: (215) 555-4805

Joseph A. Betti
1705 South 50th Street
Chicago, Illinois 60631

May 1, 1999

Mr. John H. Steven
Executive Director
Boys Club of Chicago
17065 East 110th Street
Chicago, Illinois 60630

Dear Mr. Steven:

I worked with 102 boys in 3 different youth gangs in Chicago and organized 13 different events for them.

I am writing in case you need a youth organizer for your club. If you do, you may be interested in some other things that I have done:

- As a Boy Scout, I reached the rank of Eagle Scout while still a teenager and was assigned duties as Junior Assistant Scoutmaster. I was totally responsible for 37 boys in 5 major scouting events, and assistant to the Scoutmaster in 22 other events.
- As program event chairman for my fraternity, I organized, planned, and conducted 7 major fraternity programs including a fund-raiser that raised $4,000.
- During my presidency of the University Photography Club, membership grew from 17 to 47 members. My responsibilities included supervising a club newsletter, overseeing an $82,000 photography lab, and directing the activities of 3 other club officers.
- At the university, I participated on the teams of 3 different sports and was elected captain of the tennis team.

I will be graduating in June from the University of Chicago with a B.A. degree in psychology. I would like to have a personal interview with you so we can discuss further the details of my background for this important position.

Sincerely,

Joseph A. Betti
Telephone: (312) 555-9021

Howard A. Spalding
7075 Austin Drive
Lubbock, Texas 79409

May 7, 1999

Mr. Albert A. Letz, Director
Department of Mechanical Engineering
High Technology Engineering Company
17705 Business Drive
Lubbock, Texas 79409

Dear Mr. Letz:

I designed 7 mechanical latches judged exceptional by an engineering professor with 30 years of experience.

I am writing in case you need a mechanical engineer for your department. If you do, you may be interested in some other things I've done along these lines:

- With two engineering classmates, built from scratch a special off-road vehicle that has capabilities possessed by no other vehicle in the United States.
- Designed a special device that attaches to snow shovels, increasing efficiency by 16 percent.
- Consulted for a small businessman who was trying to perfect the design of a hydraulic pump. In a special letter of commendation, he said that he could not have finished the project without my help.
- Designed a special computer program that helps design latches. This program decreases design time by approximately 22 percent.

I will be graduating with a B.S. degree in mechanical engineering from Texas Tech University at the end of May.

I would like to visit your firm and meet you in a face-to-face interview to discuss further the details of my accomplishments and experience and how they might be utilized as an engineer with your firm.

Sincerely,

Howard A. Spalding
Telephone: (806) 555-1204

Ann E. Beach
904 Book Drive
Buffalo, New York 14214

May 9, 1999

Mrs. P.C. Finch
Director
Big Library
1750 Ninth Street
Buffalo, New York 14214

Dear Mrs. Finch:

While working as a librarian's assistant at State University of New York at Buffalo, I assisted 2,112 students and 368 faculty members in library research.

I am writing in case you need an assistant librarian. If you do, here are some other things I have done that may be of interest to you:

> Cataloged more than 3,000 volumes at a major university library including classification, assignment dissection, and key word identification.
>
> Completed 2 special seminars on the use of computers in information retrieval and designed a special computer program for this purpose for medium-sized libraries as a part of a university course.
>
> Special-ordered 364 research volumes from 27 different publishers worldwide.
>
> Managed the ordering, receipt, cataloging, and replacement of 217 professional magazines subscribed to by a university library.

I will receive my B.A. degree in library science from State University of New York at Buffalo in May.

I would enjoy a personal interview to discuss further the details of my background and experience, as well as my qualifications for the position of assistant librarian.

Sincerely yours,

Ann E. Beach
Telephone: (212) 555-2897

Dana F. Brooks
757 Northern Avenue
Lincoln, Nebraska 68508

November 4, 1999

Mr. Peter W. O'Rourke
Director
Brookhaven Convalescent Home
5787 Woodrain Way
Lincoln, Nebraska 68508

Dear Mr. O'Rourke:

I developed 27 special dietary menus for individuals restricted to 9 separate diets.

I am writing in case you need a dietician for your facility. If so, you may be interested in some other things I have done:

- Completed research on the effectiveness of 9 nationally known diets given to 25,000 subjects in 31 different states.
- Worked as a part-time dietitian's assistant at Brookway Hospital, preparing dietary menus for 223 patients.
- Completed 5 longitudinal research studies on the varying effects of dietary factors on 7 subjects during a 6-month period.
- Successfully advised and assisted 13 members of my sorority with their weight problems, which resulted in an average safe weight loss of 6.25 pounds per student.

I will be graduating with a B.A. degree in home economics, with a specialty in diet analysis, from the University of Nebraska in December of this year.

I would like to meet with you to further discuss the details of my background and qualifications for the position of dietitian.

Sincerely,

Dana F. Brooks
(402) 555-2001

6

SIX

The Interview and Making the Sale

It's up to you to win the superior job by having a superior interview.

You cannot be hired without an interview, no matter how good your background, the quality of your accomplishments, or how much experience you have. You cannot be hired for any superior job without a face-to-face interview with the individual who has the authority to hire you. Therefore, the interview is the key to hiring and the only way you will be offered the job.

In previous chapters, we've discussed arranging and setting up the interview. Once this is accomplished, a new phase of groundwork begins.

Two Keys to Winning a Superior Job Offer

Preparation

In order to receive the job offer, you must be well prepared for the interview. To do this correctly requires research, planning an outline for the interview, and practice. Let's look at each in turn.

Research

Unlike your competition, you will be ready ahead of time. You will know what qualifications and accomplishments in your background are important. Also, unlike your competition, you'll stand out as an expert in the specific field in which the company is doing business.

You may wonder how to gather the necessary information. There are many sources, but your university library is the key. At the library you should get a copy of *Standard and Poor's Directory of Corporation Directors* and other references noted in Chapter Four. Try to learn the background of every individual you are likely to meet during the interview, including their colleges, employment history, honors and awards, and so forth, as well as information about the company.

When you go for the interview,
you will be an expert on that company,
its background, its product,
the general environmental situation,
and the duties of the job you are seeking.

Magazine articles in the *Wall Street Journal, Fortune, Forbes,* and other business and industry magazines are also excellent sources of information. If you do this research correctly–working right in your library–you will be able to find articles about the company, its people, products, problems, opportunities, successes, and its plans for the future.

Learn everything possible about the company in a general way. Make notes pertaining to the type of activities that may concern you, and write down any questions that will help to demonstrate your knowledge.

You can also find valuable information in annual reports, product brochures, newsletters, and other company-sponsored publications. If you are not in the same town as the company, you can request these publications by phone from its public relations or sales department. If you don't know which department provides the information you need, ask the receptionist. Usually most people are delighted to help.

If all else fails, ask the people who scheduled your interview to send the material. If you are in the same city, offer to stop by the office and pick it up. Even if your prospective boss can't furnish anything, your request demonstrates interest. Remember, doing this can only help–not hurt–your campaign to obtain a superior job.

People presently working in the company are another good source of information. Friends who have been working for the company for a few years are also an excellent source. You don't need to tell the whole situation, unless you are certain that doing so will help. Be cautious when using this source; your "friend" might make a negative comment to your prospective boss or recommend a better friend for the job you uncovered.

If you know executives who addressed students at your university, you can telephone them to ask for information about their company and about the work situation in the job you are seeking. Again, use your own judgment as to how much you should reveal to your contact. Generally, a certain amount of discretion won't hurt your case. Just tell your contact that you're looking into a job opportunity at his or her company and want to know as much about it as possible. Talk with them by telephone or arrange a face-to-face interview. If your contact thinks favorably of you, he or she might make a positive comment to your prospective boss, which will help you.

If you have heard of individuals who previously worked for the company, you can speak with them to learn more about the company and the people who run it. These individuals are especially useful for getting the hard-to-come-by facts because they are usually less inhibited than those who are currently with the company.

Another source of information is the company's competition. If you want to get information from the competition, usually the best source is someone in sales. You may call and tell them that you are a recent graduate, or a student about to graduate, and that you are seeking a job in the industry and want to know as much as you can about it. Or, you could tell them that you are actually going to interview for a job with the competition and you want to know the truth about that company from the best source you know, their strongest competitor. If you have already done your research in the library and can speak the technical jargon of the industry regarding product lines, if you know some of its personalities, and so forth, you may be able to develop a rapport with an individual in a competing company who is willing to provide all the information you want.

There is nothing unethical about this, especially if you are honest and reveal the reason you need the information. There is a remote chance that this person will be so impressed by your knowledge that you will receive an interview with the competing company as well. However, you must be particularly careful not to reveal proprietary information that may be inadvertently passed to you by employees of either company.

To conduct an interview,
your list of questions must demonstrate
your superior knowledge and your expertise.

Creating an Outline for the Interview

Having thoroughly researched your prospective employer, prepare a list of questions a superior employee would ask before taking a job. Your questions will provide the outline of the interview that *you* will conduct. Yes, I said that you will conduct the interview.

If you conduct the interview correctly, the prospective employer will seldom ask questions and will be perfectly happy to simply answer yours. Sharp, to-the-point questions demonstrate your knowledge and interest in the company and the business. This is very positive and will help to convince the interviewer that you are the best individual for the position.

I want to emphasize that your questions *must* be relevant and appropriate. Your list should not include: "What are my retirement benefits?" or "How soon can I expect a raise?" This isn't the time for such questions. Your questions must focus on the industry, the product line, and the future of the company. This demonstrates how much you know, how interested you are in the position, and that you are a *one in a thousand* expert for the job.

After you complete the interview outline, develop a list of questions that the interviewer might ask. You should expect the best, but be ready for the worst. Don't be easy on yourself. Ask tough questions, and then think of the best possible answers. You should be ready to answer the following types of questions:

Why do you think you should start at a higher level than other students in your school?

Why didn't you make better grades in school?

Why did you take so many liberal arts courses if you wanted to be in business?

Why did it take so long for you to get through school?

Why didn't you work in this industry during the summer if you were so interested?

Why didn't you take more courses having to do with this type of job, or any course having to do with this type of job?

Where do you expect to be five years from now?

Do you expect to take my job?

How much money do you think you will be worth five years from now?

Would you be willing to travel 75% or more of the time?

Would you live anywhere in the world?

Why do you want to move out of state?

Why do you really think you can do a good job in this position?

What are your three biggest strengths?

What are your three biggest weaknesses?

Will you allow your marriage to interfere with your job?

Your research of the company, the industry, and the managers of the company, should reveal other potentially embarrassing or difficult-to-answer questions. You should include them in your list and formulate answers well in advance of your interview.

Studies have shown that most questions, as many as 80 to 85 percent can be anticipated. And, of course, if you have an appropriate answer ahead of time, you'll be able to answer the question accurately and concisely.

Practice

The final step of your preparation is *practice*. You should practice or rehearse the interview by doing two things:

One, practice with the help of a wife, husband, girlfriend, boyfriend, or a friend who is sympathetic and is willing to work with you. Every phase of the interview should be practiced, everything from "Good morning" or "Good afternoon" to taking charge of the interview. I will show you how to do this shortly.

You should also practice answering the potentially embarrassing questions from the list you prepared. Let your practice interviewer think of more questions to embarrass you. Naturally, your practice interviewer should give you feedback regarding those areas in which you do well and those that need more work. You should continue to practice until your interview is polished.

Two, practice being mentally prepared for your interview. Mental preparation is much more important than you may have thought. A recent article in the *Wall Street Journal* described the work of university psychologist Dr. James Garfield. He has done research on executives in all types of industries to learn why some are effective and efficient at receiving promotions ahead of their contemporaries while others fell behind. The successful executives, he found, were able to make good presentations.

In addition, Dr. Garfield found that these above-average presentations resulted from the executives' mental preparation and rehearsal of every aspect of the presentation they were to make. This concept has been extended to sports; many experts recommend mental rehearsal of any difficult maneuver or performance before it is tested on the playing field.

After you've done the necessary research, prepared your interview outline, and practiced interviewing, you are ready to mentally prepare yourself for the interview. Before you go to bed at night, rehearse the entire interview in your mind. Picture yourself arriving at the company, knocking on the door, being asked to enter, seeing your prospective employer, being asked to sit down, taking control of the interview by asking your questions, being asked questions in turn and answering them well, and so forth. As you do this, picture everything going very well.

Mentally see how surprised and pleased your interviewer is that you know so much about the industry, the company and its products. Picture the look on his or her face clearly—the look that says you will be made an offer. And then you should picture yourself receiving the offer.

Mental rehearsal gets your psyche ready for the interview. It lessens your nervousness because you've been through it in your mind many times. Your competition, on the other hand, will be experiencing the interview for the first time. Because mental rehearsal can be done in just a few seconds, you can practice the interview ten, twenty, or thirty times in the minutes before you fall asleep. In addition to giving you more self-confidence, mental rehearsal gives you a positive attitude.

You've already *seen* yourself doing well and your prospective employer being impressed. He or she appreciated your background and experience and wanted to hire you. Mental rehearsal will have a positive affect on your ability to interview well.

Attitude

As mentioned earlier, there are two keys to winning the interview: preparation and a positive mental attitude. You should remind yourself that the interview is a learning situation. Even if you don't do well the first time, you will become better as you gain more experience. So seek a number of interviews.

Above-average presentations result from mental preparation and rehearsal of every aspect of the presentation.

Throughout the interview you should learn everything possible about the process itself. Make it a challenge to see just how well you can do. Even though the interview is a learning situation in which you have nothing to lose, it is also a sales situation. I recommend that you develop a *winning* attitude for the interview. I developed my winning attitude by playing a game. The game, very simply, is this: I interview to get a job offer from every prospective employer I meet. In other words, I want a job offer out of every single interview. I don't care if I like the company or my prospective employer. Even if I feel certain that I will ultimately turn it down, I challenge myself to obtain a superior job offer. That's what I mean by a positive, aggressive mental attitude.

The Sales Process

An interview follows a particular sequence of events: First, you arrive at the firm and are directed to your prospective employer's office. The executive may see you directly, or you may be sent to the personnel department first.

If you go to the personnel department, you will probably be given an employment form to fill out. I recommend that you take the form and start filling it out, but don't complete it. Give the bare essentials, such as your name and address. Stall as much as possible in a nice way. For example you can say, "Gee, I have a lot of this information at home. Can I take this with me to complete and send to you later?" Usually the personnel manager will agree but request that you complete as much as you can. After all, you can't be expected to furnish information you don't have available. Be especially careful *not* to indicate a range of salary that you would expect from the job. I'll discuss the reasons for this later.

Next, you'll be led to the executive's office. Observe everything. If the executive is busy, on the telephone, or not yet in the room, look around to see what his or her interests are. Look for membership certificates, awards, and so on. A trophy may indicate an interest in golf or tennis. You may have the same interest! Look for other things that you may have in common. The purpose is to find something that you can use to establish empathy with your interviewer.

It is important to establish empathy as soon as possible. Studies have shown that the decision to hire a candidate is made in the first few minutes. The remaining interview simply confirms this early judgment.

Try to build empathy based on common interests early. When your prospective employer is ready to talk with you, be prepared for a *warm-up* conversation. You may be asked about how lovely or poor the weather is, or if you had difficulty finding the place or parking, and so forth. This informal exchange is intended to relax you and the executive who is asking the questions. Do what is intended. Be relaxed and friendly. Remember that your prospective employer is not your enemy or out to get you. In fact, this is your chance to give the impression that you are an incredibly good candidate for the job.

At some point you should gently take control of the interview and go through your sequence of questions. After the first few unimportant questions, the interviewer may say something like: "Well, tell me about yourself." If you get this kind of request, smile and say, "I'll be glad to. But before I do, I wonder if I may ask a question?"

Usually there will be no problem, so you inquire, "Would you tell me the qualifications for the available position?" At that, the interviewer will usually lean back and start to tell you about the qualifications. When this happens, reach into your jacket pocket and take out the notebook containing the list of questions you prepared for the interview. Also take out a pen or pencil and begin to take notes about the important things that the executive is telling you. After all, you are being told exactly what he or she is looking for. This is extremely important information if you are to be the superior candidate for this superior job.

When the executive is finished, ask, "I wonder if you can tell me ___________" and lead into your second question. Be certain to take notes when you receive a reply. You can go through your entire list of questions in this fashion.

The key to conducting the interview is gentleness. Never try to appear pushy or overly aggressive, and always maintain your friendly attitude. If there is any balking on the part of the interviewer because you have taken control by asking questions, then retreat. After you have been asked another question, approach the interviewer with a question again. However, if the interviewer insists, back off and relinquish control.

The object is to direct the interview by asking questions first. In this way, you might not be asked any questions at all. Why? Because you have demonstrated your expertise and ability by the quality and relevance of the questions you asked.

You may wonder if the prospective employer will be offended by your note-taking during the interview. In my experience, the contrary is true. Rather than taking offense, he or she will be flattered. At the same time, you'll be noting extremely important information that will allow you to emphasize the things in your background that demonstrate your superior qualifications for the job. You can also select examples from your list of accomplishments that show how well suited you are for the different tasks that the superior job entails.

A couple of cautionary notes here. Always avoid taking a resume with you to the interview, even if it's very tempting to do so. Don't even carry one in your briefcase because you might be tempted to use it. Such temptation will only work against your best interests. Remember, a resume—even at this late stage—will expose your knock-out factors.

It will be very difficult to emphasize experience and accomplishments that were not included in your resume. It will appear that you are pulling things out of the air. On the other hand, you can always put together a specialized resume after the interview. A resume that demonstrates how well you fit the job specifications.

Another thing to avoid, at this point, is any discussion of salary. Some interviewers immediately launch into a discussion of salary requirements as soon as you sit down. They'll say, "Well, let's not mess around. How much money do you want?" or questions to this effect. You should always avoid answering. Usually, the best answer is, "Well, like you, I don't have a single figure in mind," (even though both of you might) "but, after we've talked about the job and the responsibilities, we'll have a better handle on it. I wonder if I can delay answering since I may be willing to accept less for some positions with potential; but for others, I wouldn't work for any amount of money." Usually, an answer like this will get you off the hook and delay the discussion of salary.

The reason you should delay answering salary questions is to avoid turning off your prospective employer. This person is also your customer, and, as it is with all sales, the sale should be made before money is discussed.

It's the same as when you want to buy an expensive automobile, computer, or stereo. If you know the cost up front, you might never even look at it. This is why a good real estate person will show you property at the highest price you are willing to pay, and will frequently show you something even higher. After you've seen a more expensive house and all of its desirable features, you may be willing to make additional sacrifices in order to acquire it.

It is no different when interviewing for a job. Your prospective employer may not be willing to pay the amount you want at first, but will make sacrifices elsewhere when he or she realizes just how terrific you are for the job. If your requirements are known immediately, the prospective employer may discount you before having an opportunity to learn how valuable you are.

Asking for a relatively small salary may seem like a good way to ensure that you will be offered the job you want. Many people think this, especially when they're desperate and jobs are hard to come by. But the reverse is true. If you name a figure that is too low, you may turn off your prospective employer. Why? Because he or she may have a higher figure in mind. If you mention a lower figure, the employer may think you're not qualified or that the job is too big for you to handle. Therefore, it's very important that you avoid talking about salary until after you have made the sale.

You should also avoid bringing up a discussion of fringe benefits. Wait until your prospective employer brings it up. If you ask first, it implies that you are primarily interested in the job's compensation rather than the work itself. Many employers have well-trained ears and will freeze when they hear someone ask about bonus plans, salary reviews, and vacations.

What they would really like to hear are questions about the work and job responsibilities.

However, if the employer brings up fringe benefits, it is a sign that you have made a sale. That is, your prospective employer begins to sell the job to you–he or she is already sold on you and will probably eventually make you a job offer.

Whether you are faced with one interview or many, always take control of the interview.

Throughout the interview you should remember that you are in a sales situation, and while you should be relaxed and friendly, you must keep your guard up. Be careful about discussing things that are irrelevant to your employment. I once heard about an engineer who had a job offer in his pocket, but lost it when he began a conversation that indicated his eccentric beliefs. As it happened, the prospective boss had the same eccentric beliefs but had the good sense not to mention them in his conservative workplace.

For many superior jobs, you will be required to come back for more than one interview. Sometimes you might have an interview with more than one individual. Whenever you have multiple interviews with the same individual or interviews with different individuals, you should go through the same process of preparation. Review your questions, practice, and keep notes on every interviewer and what they say.

Whether you are faced with one interview or many, always take control of the interview and when it is completed you should look at your interviewer and say something like: "I've really enjoyed this interview and I like your company. I would like to work for you." If you have other offers going at the same time, don't be afraid to tell the interviewer. This is especially true if you are to give the others a yes or no answer by a certain time. You want to put the pressure on your prospective employer–not on you.

You can do this very easily by simply saying, "I really enjoyed the interview and I would like to work for your company, but I have to tell you this. I have two other offers right now and I must answer them by Friday. I hope that you will make a job offer, because I want to work for you. Can you give me your answer by Thursday?"

Many job candidates fail to put this pressure on their prospective employers. They feel if they reveal negotiations with another company that the prospective employer will be offended. In most cases, however, the contrary is true. If you are known to be in demand and desirable, the employer will want you even more, and, if there is pressure on him to act, he will be more inclined to make an offer sooner. After all, would you turn down a superior candidate simply because someone else was interested? Would you let this superior candidate slip through your fingers simply because you want to diddle-daddle around?

What you want to avoid is letting the interview end with someone saying, "Well, we'll let you know. We would like to see a few more candidates." Then the prospective employer has you dangling on a string. If you're put in this position, turn it around by saying, "I really would like to work for you, but I have to tell you that I have other offers. Can you please finish with the other interviews and get back with me as soon as possible?"

If you do this, your prospective employer may not even bother with anyone else. If you've done your work well, you are a superior candidate for the superior job. Your prospective employer would have to be a fool not to make you an offer. And you do not want other candidates to be seen—it's just not in your best interest. It's better to beat the competition out before they even get up to bat.

As soon as you are offered the job, you have the advantage. In general, it's best *not* to accept the job offer at once, unless you are 100 percent sure. The company has committed itself and you now have the job in your pocket. It is very rare for a company to withdraw an offer once it has been made; unless, of course, you don't accept the job within the agreed upon period of time.

After the offer has been made, say something like: "I appreciate this very much. I wonder if I could have a week or so to think it over." This is important even if you don't have another offer to consider. One may come that is better, and you certainly would not decline a job once you accept it. It's possible to get away with changing your mind, but it's very embarrassing, very tricky, and potentially damaging to your reputation in the industry. It's easier to ask for time to think things over, weigh all the pluses and minuses on your own, and decide clearly whether this particular job is the one for you.

I recently heard from a student who had just received her MBA from a major school and wanted very much to be a management consultant with a major company. She conducted her campaign as recommended. She called and said, "Well, I followed your advice and got the offer but did not accept it, and my husband was very mad at me because it's more money than he's making as an engineer."

"How much was it?" I asked.

"Forty-thousand dollars," she said.

Well, $40,000 is a lot of money, so I could understand why her husband was angry. But I asked her, "Well, tell me what happened, and what are your plans?"

"Well," she said, "I wondered, since they offered $40,000, if I couldn't get even more."

I acknowledged that if they had opened with $40,000, then it was possible to get even more. " Tell me everything," I said.

She told me the whole story: "I followed the campaign, and I'd been going on a series of different interviews, and this one was firm. They called me in and made the offer face-to-face at $40,000. I told them that I would really like to work for them but that I had two other offers in the high forties and therefore would have to think it over. I asked for a couple of days. They granted me the delay," she said, "and I have to go in tomorrow with my decision."

"Okay," I said, "you've handled things just right. When you go in tomorrow, tell them you thought it over and that you really want to work for their firm, which I assume that you do."

"Yes," my former student answered, "I do."

"Tell them that you thought it over and that you really would like to work for them but that one of the other offers is $47,500. Ask if they can meet that offer."

"There are only three things they can do," I said, "one is they'll come back with $47,500. But this is rather unlikely since $40,000 places you in the upper half of 1 percent for MBA students graduating this year. The other possibility is that they'll say no, there's no way of meeting the offer. In that case you can just say, okay, I really want to work for you, and I'll take the $40,000. But it's most likely that they will attempt to negotiate somewhere between $40,000 and $47,500. So, good luck," I said and sent her on her way.

The following evening she called me. "Well," she said, "you were absolutely right. I went in and told them that the other offer was at $47,500, and they immediately countered at $45,000.

"In fact," she said, "I think that's when I made my only mistake, because I jumped up and practically shouted, *I'll take it!* But at any rate, my husband's not mad any longer, and I'm starting next week at $45,000 a year."

If your first interview didn't result in a job offer, you need to tie up the sales process by writing a post-interview letter. A post-interview letter is not just a little note saying thank you for the interview. After all, they have just as much reason to thank you for the interview as you have to thank them.

Your post-interview letter
is your opportunity to review
all of your qualifications for the superior job.

The notes you made during the interview will tell you which aspects of your background to highlight. For every qualification noted during the interview, you should list four or five accomplishments that demonstrate your superiority over any possible competition for that particular aspect of the job. Then, at the end of the letter, you should say, "I would really like to work for you, and I think your company is outstanding and offers a great deal of potential for hard workers." Sign it, and again put your telephone number at the end of the letter.

You've now done all you can, and the next move is up to the company. If you don't hear from them within a week or two, you should call the interviewer on the telephone. Tell your prospective boss again that you want to work for him or her and how well qualified for the job you consider yourself to be. It is never wrong to call or write the company in question and ask for the offer. Put yourself in their position. Would you be mad at a superior candidate simply because he or she called and wanted to work for you?

No, on the contrary. The only time that you would lose out under such circumstances is if you were never really considered a prime candidate. If you are not a real candidate, the sooner you know it, the sooner you can move on to better things. But if you *are* a strong candidate, contacting them to express your interest in the job will not turn them off from wanting to hire you—a great candidate for a great job.

Now you know all that is necessary to land a superior job. Good luck!

About the Author

Dr. William A. Cohen, Chairman of the Department of Marketing, California State University, Los Angeles, has held a number of senior management positions in industry, served as a corporation president, been an executive recruiter and, while Director of the Small Business Institute, supervised consulting for more than 300 small businesses. Additionally he serves on several boards of directors and consults for Fortune 500 companies.

Among his 12 books and more than 100 professional papers is the highly successful *The Executive's Guide to Finding a Superior Job,* which has sold in excess of 40,000 copies. A number of his books, including *Direct Response Marketing, Building a Mail Order Business* (a business bestseller), *Winning on the Marketing Front,* and *High Tech Management,* have been translated into Japanese, German, Norwegian, Danish, and Finnish.

Dr. Cohen is the recipient of the Freedom Foundation, a Valley Forge George Washington Honor Medal for Excellence in Economic Education, and the President's Medal for Merit. His numerous other awards and fellowships include the Outstanding Professor's Award at California State University, Los Angeles—only the second business professor to receive this prestigious award in its 20-year history. Many regional, national, and international directories, as well as *Who's Who in America,* include Dr. Cohen's biography.

His educational background includes a B.S. in engineering from the United States Military Academy, an MBA from the University of Chicago and an M.A. and Ph.D. in management from Claremont Graduate School. A member of the Beta Gamma Sigma honorary business fraternity, Dr. Cohen is also a member of the American Marketing Association, the Direct Marketing Association, the European Marketing Academy, and a Fellow of the Academy of Marketing Science.